The Master Detective Handbook

Janice Eaton Kilby

Illustrated by
Jason Chin

Help Our Detectives
Use Gadgets & Super
Sleuthing Skills to
Solve the Mystery
& Catch the Crooks

LARK BOOKS
A Division of Sterling Publishing Co., Inc.
New York / London

Editor:
Rain Newcomb

Creative Director:
Celia Naranjo

Illustration:
Jason Chin

Technical Illustration:
Orrin Lundgren

Art Production Assistant:
Bradley Norris

Editorial Assistance:
Rose McLarney and
Delores Gosnell

The Library of Congress has cataloged the hardcover edition as follows:

Kilby, Janice Eaton, 1955-
  The master detective handbook : help our detectives use gadgets & super sleuthing skills to solve the mystery & catch the crooks / by Janice Eaton Kilby ; illustrated by Jason Chin.
     p. cm.
  Includes index.
  ISBN 1-57990-849-7 (hardcover)
  1. Handicraft—Juvenile literature. 2. Detectives—Juvenile literature.
3. Detective and mystery stories—Juvenile literature. I. Title.
TT160.K4746 2006
363.25028'4—dc22

                                    2006014279

10 9 8 7 6 5 4 3 2 1

Published by Lark Books, A Division of
Sterling Publishing Co., Inc.
387 Park Avenue South, New York, N.Y. 10016

First Paperback Edition 2008
Text © 2006, Lark Books
Illustrations © 2006, Jason Chin

Distributed in Canada by Sterling Publishing,
c/o Canadian Manda Group, 165 Dufferin Street
Toronto, Ontario, Canada M6K 3H6

Distributed in the United Kingdom by GMC Distribution Services,
Castle Place, 166 High Street, Lewes, East Sussex, England BN7 1XU

Distributed in Australia by Capricorn Link (Australia) Pty Ltd.,
P.O. Box 704, Windsor, NSW 2756 Australia

If you have questions or comments about this book, please contact:
Lark Books
67 Broadway
Asheville, NC 28801
(828) 253-0467

Manufactured in China

ISBN 13: 978-1-57990-849-2 (hardcover) 978-1-60059-290-4 (paperback)
ISBN 10: 1-57990-849-7 (hardcover) 1-60059-290-2 (paperback)

For information about custom editions, special sales, premium and corporate purchases, please contact Sterling Special Sales Department at 800-805-5489 or specialsales@sterlingpub.com.

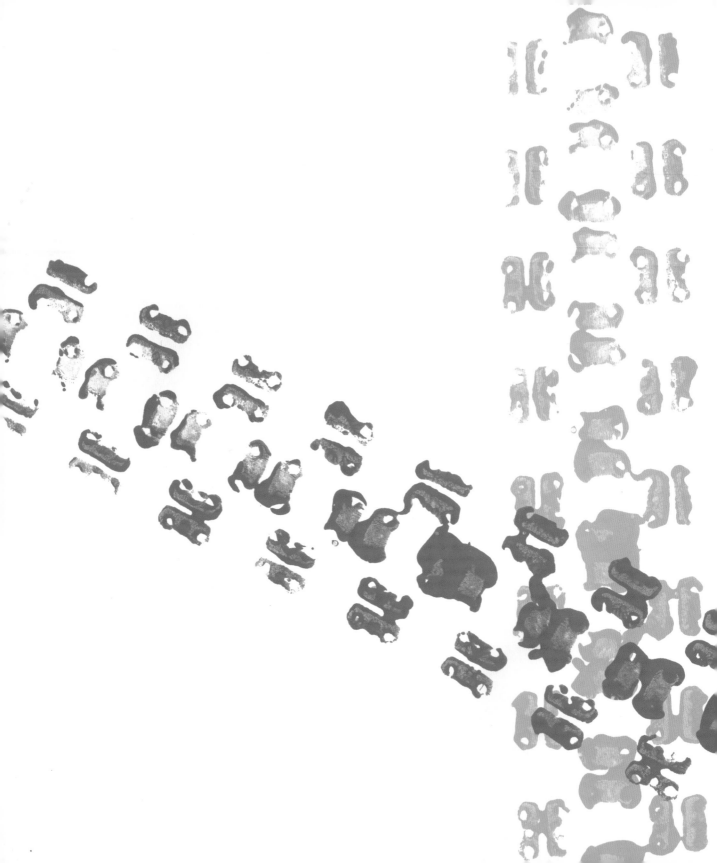

The Master Detective Handbook

Dear Budding Detective,

What do you get when you have three sleuths, one fat dog named Sam Spayed, a missing friend, and vanishing grades at school? And what do video games and a hamburger company have to do with it, anyway? It's a mystery!

How did it all start? I was alone, toiling away at my typewriter late one night when—

Knock. Knock. Knock. Woof!

Through the peephole of my front door, I spied a red-headed gal, two guys, and an overweight bloodhound. They claimed to be detectives from the Pink Pinkerton Agency. Said they'd heard I was a writer, and they needed my help to tell their story. I agreed, but then I had to referee. They were all strongly opinionated people with something to say. So I convinced them to take turns telling what happened.

Are their arch-nemeses, Suzye Sylk and her evil gang of two, involved? Will our three friends manage to save Cyn City from a terrible fate? Will they still get a ride to school in the morning?

Just to make it fun, you're not going to learn "who done it" all at once. You'll get plenty of chances to take note of significant clues and solve the mystery yourself. And you'll learn how to be a good detective along the way. You'll find instructions for making the Pink Pinkerton Detective Agency's favorite detecting tools, and be able to practice using the techniques that detectives use to nab the bad guy. All the things Pink and her gang wanted to tell you about couldn't fit in this book, so at the very end you'll find a handbook full of tricks and tips for your own detective work.

So put on your detecting hat and join us! Have fun. And do good.

Happy Sleuthing,

Janice

How to Use This Book

While you read the story and solve the mystery, you'll learn how to make useful things for your own detecting work. Look for notes that'll show you how to make cool devices and practice your detective skills. Pink's notes are (you guessed it) pink. Homes' notes are on steno paper, and Hu's notes are on one of his electronic devices. This symbol 🔍 will alert you to look for footnotes with more information—if you can find them, heh heh. Keep your magnifying glass handy! (Many people in this world do not automatically read from top to bottom or left to right. But we're not saying any more about that. You're the detective.)

As you're unraveling the mystery, you'll come across some codes. Detectives (and the criminals they follow) frequently communicate via coded messages, and you'll have the chance to solve the codes in this book. Use the hints to get started cracking the codes. If you get stumped, turn to page 95.

Starting on page 77, you'll find a copy of the Pink Pinkerton Detective Agency's Handbook. In it, you'll find even more techniques to try and things to make.

CHAPTER 1

Our Gang

Ellen "Pink" Pinkerton. Hi! So you want to be a detective, too, huh? I'm the great-great-great-great-granddaughter of Allen Pinkerton, the famous Scottish immigrant who started the first American detective agency. My friends call me Pink. So I decided, don't fight it, embrace it! I started the Pink Pinkerton Agency with my two best friends, Sherman Homes and Mike Hu. Oh, and this is my dog, Sam Spayed.

Homes and Hu are the brainiest guys I know. Homes idolizes Sherlock Holmes and even talks like him: By Jove! But you get used to it. Hu is the coolest. You'd never guess all the gruesome (but useful) information he carries around in his head. And if he doesn't already know it, he can find it. We detect whenever we can, as long as we stay under the parents' radar and get our homework done.

Sherman Homes. My brain is my best weapon. We've foresworn violence in the execution of our duties, so it's handy I'm an expert in aikido, the self-defense art. You use your opponent's energies to send him sailing away, embarrassed.

I'd stay in my room for months, if my parents let me. And what's the point in cleaning up? That's not lazy, that's a focused use of my energies.

Mike Hu, aka Doctor Hu. Yeah, everybody christened me Doctor Hu when they found out I have an encyclopedic memory for spectacular crimes. The grosser, the better! Did you know you can check for poison by analyzing a person's liver since it filters nasty stuff from the blood? Unfortunately, the person has to be (ahem) dead for you to do that.

But I'm not all about gore. I'm more like the famous detective Poirot. We both love to eat (hamburgers for me!) and use our "little grey cells" (brains) to solve the mystery.

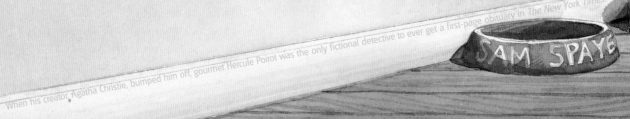

When his creator, Agatha Christie, bumped him off, gourmet Hercule Poirot was the only fictional detective to ever get a first-page obituary in *The New York Times*.

Pink. We live in Canyon City. The canyons are mostly suburbs now, connected by cars in between. We call it Cyn City (soft c, short i, like in pill) even though Cyn City is the kind of town where you go to the mall and watch the fountains drip or hang out at Burp! Burgers. S-o-o boring.

Make Your Own Detective Agency Sign

When we started the agency, the first thing I did was make a sign for my door. Otherwise, how would clients find me? Here's a copy of great-great-great-great granddad's famous 'eye' that you can use.

WHAT YOU NEED

- Photocopier or tracing paper and pencil
- Black marker
- Scissors
- White glue
- Stiff cardboard or foam core, approximately 8 x 11 inches
- Art supplies
- Piece of string
- Masking tape

WHAT YOU DO

1. Photocopy the template above or use the tracing paper and pencil to trace it. When you enlarge the template, make it a size that fits the piece of cardboard and still leaves some room for writing.

2. Use your artistic talents to add l-o-n-g eyelashes to the eye, color to the image, or any other details you like. Go over all the lines with the black marker to make them more prominent.

3. Cut out the picture and glue it to the cardboard, smoothing it flat. Let it dry.

4. Write your agency's name on the sign or include helpful phrases, such as MASTER PEEPER or CRIMES SOLVED HERE or THE DETECTIVE IS IN.

5. Decorate the picture as you wish. I glued lavender glitter eye shadow and long, cut-out construction paper eyelashes to my eye!

6. Tape the string to the back of the sign and hang it on your door.

But weird stuff happens beneath the surface of our little burb—like when our friend Hack disappeared. I liked Hack, even if he did keep sending me illegal music files. He could hack into any computer system invented. (I'm probably going to have to arrest him when I get older.) But he was gone, bad things were happening, and we were the only detective agency in town, so it was up to us to find out why. Well, at least we were the only ones with a really cool sign.

Pink. I was at home when I got a phone call from Hu. "Everyone's grades have been erased from the school computer!" he said. "And my parents are so upset! They've planned on me going to MIT since I was two."

Then an email arrived from Homes. It was in code, or cipher, as he'd say. Homes can be so fussy sometimes. I decoded the email. Time to grab the crime kit!

Make Your Own Crime Kit

A good gumshoe always keeps her crime kit ready. You need a kit like this to collect evidence. Keep it well-stocked and on hand.

WHAT YOU NEED

- Shoebox, toolbox, or small suitcase
- Smaller boxes to fit into large box
- Package of clothing elastic or velcro tape, available in fabric stores
- Craft glue
- Protective clothing: long-sleeved shirt, rubber gloves, shower cap, and bandanna or face mask
- Measuring tape
- Dollar bill (see page 21)
- Sketchpad
- Pen or pencil
- Camera (throwaway or cheapie digital is fine.)
- Flashlight (mini-sized if you have one)
- Magnifying glass
- Cotton swabs and balls
- Roll of clear packing tape, 2 inches wide
- Masking tape
- Ball of string
- Scissors
- Tweezers
- Clean, empty pill bottles, plastic baggies, and small paper envelopes

WHAT YOU DO

1. Pick out the largest box. This will be the outside of your kit. Label it with your name and an identifier, such as DETECTION SUPPLIES.

2. Arrange the smaller boxes inside the kit to make compartments. Glue them in place. If you keep the lids on, label them with the names of the contents: STRING, COTTON, etc.

3. Make convenient stay-put holders for small instruments—such as the pencil, scissors, and tweezers—by gluing short pieces of the elastic inside the lid. Lay the lid flat on a work surface. Cut the elastic into 2-inch lengths. Apply the glue to both ends, but leave the middle unglued so you'll have a space to slip the tool through. Press the elastic in place and let it dry. (You can use the velcro tape instead. Stick one side to the tool and one side to the lid.)

4. Cover the pill bottle labels with masking tape so you'll have a blank place to label any evidence collected.

5. Arrange small or heavy items in the box compartments. The kit items are roughly in the order you'd use them at the scene. Lay the protective clothing items on top. You're ready for action!

Technically, you make a cipher by replacing letters or numbers with substitute symbols. Entire words or phrases are replaced to make a code.

Pink. I pondered Homes' note as I grabbed my detective jacket. We didn't want to call the police—not yet. We had to find Hack before anyone blamed him for the grades meltdown. Somebody had hacked into the school computer system, and I hoped that somebody wasn't Hack. It would have been easy for him to break into the system—he is a hacker after all. If he was guilty, maybe we could convince him to fix it. And if it didn't get fixed, I thought, forget college. A lifetime of "Do you want fries with that?" at Burp! Burgers wasn't something I looked forward to.

Best-Dressed Detective Jacket

A good detective always knows where her tools are. Make a jacket that won't draw attention to you and gives you quick access to your tools.

WHAT YOU NEED

- Front-opening jacket with a front chest pocket
- Flashlight
- Clothing elastic, 1 inch wide
- Straight pins
- Needle
- Thread
- Measuring tape
- Scissors
- Magnifying glass

WHAT YOU DO

1. Measure the circumference of the flashlight. Cut two pieces of elastic to that length.

2. Pin the pieces of elastic inside the jacket, one above the other. Sew the ends to the jacket. The loops should be snug enough to keep the flashlight head from slipping through.

3. Repeat steps 1 and 2 to make holding loops for the magnifying glass.

Secret Camera Pocket

Add this pocket to your detective jacket so that you can take photographs secretly.

WHAT YOU NEED

- Measuring tape
- Disposable camera
- Scissors
- Large piece of fabric
- Self-adhesive velcro tape, 1 inch wide
- Piece of chalk
- Fabric glue
- Safety pins
- Jacket
- Bandanna

WHAT YOU DO

1. Measure the camera. Cut a rectangle of fabric at least two and a half times as tall and one and a half times as long as the camera is. It should be big enough to slip your hand into when the fabric is folded over the camera.

2. Cut two pieces of velcro, each as long as the camera. Peel away the backing on one side of the velcro and stick it to the back of the camera. Repeat with the second piece of velcro. Make sure you don't cover any important buttons.

3. Lay the fabric flat on a work surface, its longest side running from top to bottom. Fold the fabric in half the long way and mark where the fold line is on the inside of the fabric with the chalk. Remove the rest of the backing from the tape. Put the camera (taped side down) in the center of the fabric above the fold line. Press the camera firmly into place.

4. Unhook the camera. (Half of the tape should stay on the fabric.) Fold the fabric over to make a pocket. Glue the top and right edge of the fabric together. (If you're left handed, glue the left edge of the fabric.) You'll use the open edge of the pocket to put your hand through. Let the glue dry.

5. Put the camera in the pocket, pressing it against the velcro to hold it in place. Draw a circle on the fabric around the camera lens with the chalk. Remove the camera, and then snip a hole in the fabric so that the camera can see. Put the camera back in place.

6. Position the pocket inside the jacket so that the camera lens will be against the jacket. If you're right-handed, put the lens behind the left front pocket of the jacket (beneath the top edge of the chest pocket on the outside of the jacket). If you're left-handed, do the opposite. Pin the pocket in place. Mark its position on the inside of the jacket with the chalk.

7. Feel from the outside of the jacket to determine where the lens is. Use chalk to mark the position. Remove the camera pocket and snip a hole big enough so the camera can see.

8. Put the pocket back inside the jacket, using the chalk marks you made in step 6. Check that the lens will be properly positioned when the camera is stuck to the tape.

9. Put the bandanna in the outside pocket, covering the camera hole with the ends.

10. To take a picture, slip your right hand into the fabric pocket, lift up the bandanna with your left hand, and press the button.

Chapter 2

The Scene of the Crime

Hu. Hack was older than us and already had his driver's license, lucky dog. Sometimes he gave us a ride to school on his way to Canyon City High. But his puke-green 1965 Ford, The Malteaser Falcon,  was parked at the curb outside his house. It was the only thing Hack loved as much as the malted milk candy he was always eating. We could hear calliope music coming from Hack's bedroom, but nobody answered our knock. The door was unlocked. So naturally we went in. The room was trashed more than normal: Burp! Burgers wrappers everywhere, video game holders open and scattered. Hack's favorite T-shirt, the one that never left his body, lay on the floor, along with the Action Man that usually hung from a noose over his computer. But the A-Man was no more. He'd been chopped into pieces. And Hack was gone.

Calliope music is most commonly heard at the circus

16

Memory Master:
Noticing and Remembering Details

Good detection requires acute powers of observation, and you're going to test yours. Turn back to the picture of Hack's room on page 16. Study it for 30 seconds, making special note of anything you think is important, and then turn back to this page.

Write down everything you remember seeing, without looking at the picture.

Now, write down your answers to these questions. No peeking.

- What's on the floor?
- What's on Hack's bed?
- What's on the walls?
- What's on the desk?
- What's on the ceiling?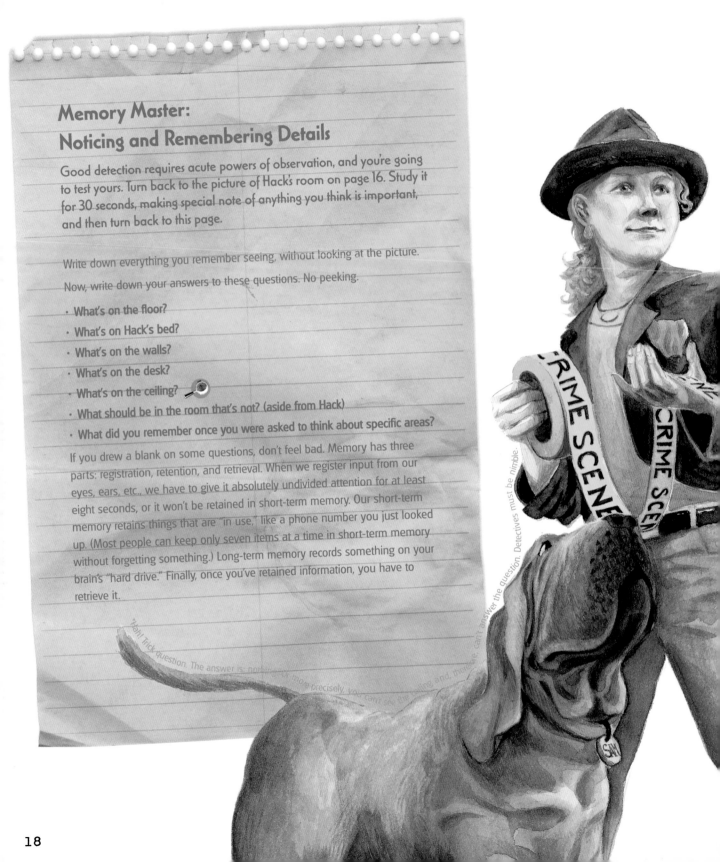
- What should be in the room that's not? (aside from Hack)
- What did you remember once you were asked to think about specific areas?

If you drew a blank on some questions, don't feel bad. Memory has three parts: registration, retention, and retrieval. When we register input from our eyes, ears, etc., we have to give it absolutely undivided attention for at least eight seconds, or it won't be retained in short-term memory. Our short-term memory retains things that are "in use," like a phone number you just looked up. (Most people can keep only seven items at a time in short-term memory without forgetting something.) Long-term memory records something on your brain's "hard drive." Finally, once you've retained information, you have to retrieve it.

Hah! Trick question. The answer is: nothing — or, more precisely, you can't see the ceiling and, therefore, can't answer the question. Detectives must be nimble.

Homes. We stood at the door, gazing at the chaos. Pink immediately ran crime scene tape (see page 80) back and forth across the door, taping it in place. We had to note everything at the scene carefully before disturbing the evidence by entering the room. Here was our chance to imagine what might have happened, where an intruder would have entered and left the room, and what had been taken—or left behind. A true detective hones his memory just for situations like this.

Sharpening Your Memory

It's actually really easy to exercise your memory muscles. (This is my favorite way to exercise.)

1. Vary your habits to make your brain use new pathways. If you're left-handed, brush your teeth with your right hand. Close your eyes while you take a shower. If you walk to school, take a different route.

2. Write down the license plate numbers of all the cars on your street. See if you can remember the numbers the next time you see the car.

3. If you're learning a list of things, set it to a tune and sing it. Or, make up an acronym, a word composed of the first letters of all the words on the list.

4. Draw a map of your neighborhood, with landmarks and streets. Now take a walk and see what you left out. (This will be useful later when you're tailing someone.)

5. Shuffle a deck of cards and spread them out on the floor. Pick up two at a time, look at them, and put them face-down on the floor. Draw two more cards. If you get a match (you drew a queen and have drawn a second one), try to remember where you laid the first one and put the second on top.

6. Eat orange, red, blue, and deep green fruits and veggies. They have vitamins and antioxidants that feed the brain. Think tomatoes, berries, cabbage (OK, maybe not that last one).

Hu. The first things I noticed were footprints on the floor: clear heel and sole marks that tracked in and out of the room. But it was their size that stunned me. Each print was 8 inches wide and 2 feet long from heel to toe. The owner of the feet was a giant! Do you realize how tall he'd be? (See page 31.) Had Bigfoot snatched Hack? I have a file on him, although Homes always scoffs at my "urban legends." But I'd never read about Bigfoot wearing shoes. Plenty of time for speculation later—I needed to record the scene, making a detailed account of everything that was in Hack's room and precisely where it was.

★ Hu's Email   File   Edit   View   Mailbox   Format   Message   Window   Help

Send   Attach   Addresses   *F* Fonts   Colors

To: pink@pinkpinkertonagency.com

CC: sherman@pinkpinkertonagency.com

Subject: Project

Record the Scene: Make a Photo Scale

Your own room is too familiar, so practice your recording skills on a friend's room. I practiced on Homes' room. That guy never cleans, but he knows precisely where everything is.

WHAT YOU NEED

- Camera
- Adhesive mailbox numbers*
- Dollar bill
- Pencil
- Tablet of paper

*Available at hardware stores.

WHAT YOU DO

1. Take photos of the room. Shoot from the four corners (to show overall layout) and at mid-range (to show the relationship of key pieces of evidence and items in the room).

2. Take close-ups of visible prints and key pieces of evidence, putting a mailbox number in each shot. Shoot each item alone first, and then with the dollar bill. (This will help you remember how big the item is later.) Keep a running list of photos, including the subject matter and purpose of each shot.

3. Sketch the room as if you're looking straight down from the ceiling. Add room dimensions. (Measure one of your feet, and then walk heel-to-toe across the room. Multiply the number of steps you took by your foot length to get the room dimensions.)

4. Add doors, windows, and furniture to the sketch, marking sizes and distances in between.

5. Add evidence numbers. For example, if you photographed a bottle with mailbox marker number 3, put the number 3 in your drawing where you found the bottle.

In Dorothy Sayers' *Unnatural Death*, Lord Peter Wimsey pursues a mystery villain who leaves three different sets of footprints.

21

Homes. Hack was no housekeeper—but neither am I. You could see dust tracks on the bookshelves where all his games had been pulled out. There were smeared finger marks on the walls and a clear set of handprints, right and left hands, about 5 feet apart, where the intruder had stretched out his arms. The hands were monstrous, just like the feet, with fingers like dinner sausages and palms as big as salad plates. Who was this colossus of crime, this Mister Big of Burglary? Sadly, my efforts to collect prints  failed. There were only smudges. But that told me something important: Mr. Big had worn gloves.

Fingerprint Kit

Keep this handy box in your detective kit so that you can lift a print whenever you need to.

WHAT YOU NEED

- Shoebox or lunch box
- 2 small, clean jars with lids
- Loose, pale ladies' face powder or talcum powder
- Cocoa or instant coffee powder
- 2 new, clean, long-bristle makeup brushes or feathers
- Index cards and black construction paper

WHAT YOU DO

1. Fill one of the jars with the face or talcum powder.
2. Fill the other with the cocoa or coffee powder.
3. Put the index cards and construction paper flat on the bottom of the box.
4. Put the jars in the box with the makeup brushes and the clear tape.

Mark Twain was the first American writer to note fingerprints' importance. The plot of *The Tragedy of Pudd'nhead Wilson* turns on them.

22

Dusting for Fingerprints

Dusting for fingerprints is easy, once you've put together your Fingerprint Kit. Here's how:

WHAT YOU NEED
- Mirror, framed picture, or glass tabletop
- Flashlight
- Fingerprint kit
- Camera
- Clear tape, 2 inches wide
- Black construction paper
- Magnifying glass with 3x or 4x power
- Glass cleaner
- Clean rag

Plain Arch   Tented Arch

Radial Loop   Ulnar Loop

Plain Whorl   Central Pocket Loop

WHAT YOU DO

1. Check the mirror, picture, or glass tabletop for prints by shining the flashlight at an angle from the side.

2. When you find a fingerprint, get out your fingerprint kit.

3. Make a small pile of the light-colored powder. Touch the makeup brush to it, then gently brush the powder from side to side over the print. When visible ridges appear, gently blow away excess powder.

4. When you're lifting a fingerprint from a light-colored surface, use the dark powder. When you're lifting a print from a dark-colored surface, use the light powder. Always keep your brushes clean, and never mix the powders on one brush.

5. Photograph the print. Then smooth a piece of tape over it. Lift the tape. Stick it to an index card or the construction paper. (Lift light prints onto black and dark prints onto white papers.) Initial and date them.

6. Use the magnifying glass and the fingerprint chart above to identify unique points on the prints. Compare them to your Fingerprint Database (see page 81). See anyone you know?

7. Clean the mirror, picture, or glass tabletop with the glass cleaner and rag when you're done.

Homes. Hack's bed was its usual unmade mess. On the pillow lay a small piece of paper, with mismatched cut-and-paste letters stuck to it.

Sore? Was Hack hurt? Angry? Why hadn't he used his computer to make the note? I whipped out my magnifying glass. I recognized the fonts and colors that made up the mystery note. They all came from slick video game magazines.

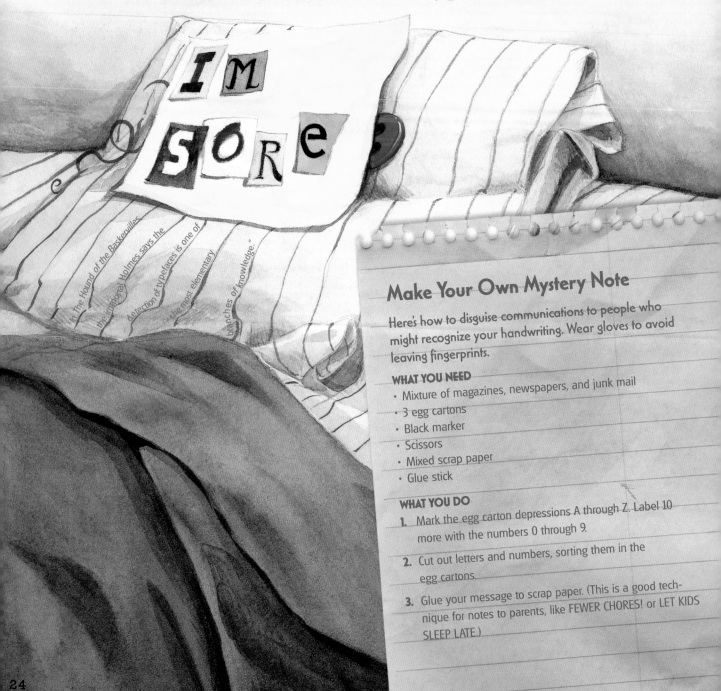

In the Hound of the Baskervilles, the immortal Holmes says the detection of typefaces is one of the most elementary branches of knowledge.

Make Your Own Mystery Note

Here's how to disguise communications to people who might recognize your handwriting. Wear gloves to avoid leaving fingerprints.

WHAT YOU NEED
- Mixture of magazines, newspapers, and junk mail
- 3 egg cartons
- Black marker
- Scissors
- Mixed scrap paper
- Glue stick

WHAT YOU DO
1. Mark the egg carton depressions A through Z. Label 10 more with the numbers 0 through 9.
2. Cut out letters and numbers, sorting them in the egg cartons.
3. Glue your message to scrap paper. (This is a good technique for notes to parents, like FEWER CHORES! or LET KIDS SLEEP LATE.)

Pink. While Homes examined the note, I checked the pillow for trace evidence. It had longish, bright red, fuzzy hairs stuck to it. Interesting. Hack had short brown hair. And next to the hairs was a giant button, 3 inches wide. I tweezered it into an evidence bag and sealed it up (see page 78).

Collecting Trace Evidence: Hair and Fiber

We shed trace—hair, fibers, and dirt—all the time. With thorough collection and good analysis, trace can tell you who's been in a room and where he was before that.

WHAT YOU NEED

- Clothing
- Large sheet of white paper
- Butter knife
- Envelopes
- Flashlight
- Clear package tape, 2 inches wide
- Vacuum cleaner with clean bag
- Pencil
- Scissors
- Magnifying glass or microscope
- Tweezers

WHAT YOU DO

1. Hang the clothing above the paper. Scrape it with the knife. Stow the trace you knock off in the envelopes.

2. Hold the flashlight at an angle to the floor. Experiment with the angle until the dust and dirt on the floor show up. Use the package tape to pick up the trace.

3. Vacuum the house. Remember what order you vacuum the rooms in. Slit the bag lengthwise. See layers? Each layer of trace came from a particular room in your house. Trace can help you identify where someone (or something) has been.

4. Use the magnifying glass and tweezers to examine the hairs and fibers you collected. Hairs and fibers can tell you more about your suspect. Pay attention to the length, color, curliness, texture, thickness, tip, and root of each hair. Carpet has longer and thicker fibers than clothing.

5. Tape samples to a piece of paper and label their probable origin.

"Everything may depend on the difference between two hairs." — Chinese Proverb

Pink. I used my flashlight to examine the wall from an angle, to see if our goon had left any other interesting marks. Maybe there was something behind the MegaTrash and Screaming Clowns black light posters on the walls. So I peeled them away. Nothing. Then I saw it! The light was shining through little holes poked in the posters, like Hack had used them for target practice. The holes traced two words:

T R A S H   C L O W N

My extensive background in projectile analysis immediately told me that Hack made his mark(s) by throwing darts into his poster. He must have been sitting in his computer chair while he did it. Good thing Hack has great aim.

The String's the Thing: Spatter and Projectile Analysis

This is one of my favorite activities: you get to have fun making a mess, and if any grown-up wonders what you're doing, you can tell him you're "furthering your education" and "learning how to predict the origin point of spatters."

WHAT YOU NEED

- Clothesline or rope
- 2 trees or poles
- Old sheet
- Clothespins
- Cornstarch
- Water
- Cold cream
- Measuring spoons
- Small bowl
- Food coloring
- Fork
- A friend
- Paintbrush
- Ball of string
- Straight pins
- Dowels or twigs
- Scissors

WHAT YOU DO

1. Tie the clothesline between two trees or poles. Pin the sheet to it.

2. Put 8 teaspoons cornstarch, 4 tablespoons water, 4 tablespoons cold cream, and 8 drops of food coloring in the bowl. Mix with the fork.

3. Your friend should leave the area. Pick a place at least five feet away from the sheet. Discretely mark the spot on the ground.

4. Standing on that spot, dip the brush in one of the paints. Flick it toward the sheet. Make six or eight spatters.

5. Move away from the spot, bring your friend back, and have him guess where you were standing.

6. In order to figure out the "point of origin" for the spatters (which is where you were standing), pin one end of the string to a spatter mark. Unwind the ball of string, holding it so that it makes a line from the spatter to where you think the point of origin is. Cut the string and tie the other end to a dowel. Stick the dowel in the ground at the point of origin.

7. Test out your guess by repeating step 6 on another spatter. The more spatters you analyze like this, the more likely you are to pinpoint the exact point of origin.

Hu. It was cold, really cold, what someone had done to Hack's Action Man. (To promote their new video games, BaddBoyz gave away an Action Man and a free screen saver every time you bought a Burp! Burger.) A-Man felt warm to the touch, lying there on the floor. His head—and arms, and legs—had been torn off. You might say this was a case of, ah, armed robbery. I also noticed several large, brown, sticky drops scattered around the body. Could it be blood?

When a mammal expires, it stops creating heat and its temperature drops about a degree and a half every hour. Action Man was plastic, of course. But the BB logo on his torso was a little faded, like he'd been lying in the sun for several days. Sunlight heats what it hits, and it causes chemical bonds of materials to change. Knowing the local conditions, I might be able to deduce how long he'd been lying there.

Send   **Attach**   **Addresses**   **Fonts**   **Colors**

To: pink@pinkpinkertonagency.com

CC: sherman@pinkpinkertonagency.com

Subject: Project

Recording Local Conditions

You can figure out how much time has elapsed since the crime was committed by knowing how sunlight affects different objects. Here's how to collect that information.

WHAT YOU NEED
- 4-inch squares, two each of black construction paper, colored cloth, and colored plastic
- 3 jar lids
- Camera

WHAT YOU DO

1. To figure out how sunlight affects different objects, position the squares of paper, cloth, and plastic in a protected, consistently sunny spot in your house. Put a jar lid on one of each pair of squares, positioning the other square beside it and uncovered.

2. Check under the lids every half-hour, for four hours, noting changes in the material underneath the jar. Photograph the results. Check them the next day, too.

3. The chemical bonds between paper dye and the paper weaken when exposed to the sun, so you'll be able to use this information to estimate how long ago an object was placed in the position you found it.

Hu. I scraped up some flakes from the brown spots on Hack's floor. Some were large, round drops, like they'd fallen from a bloody nose. 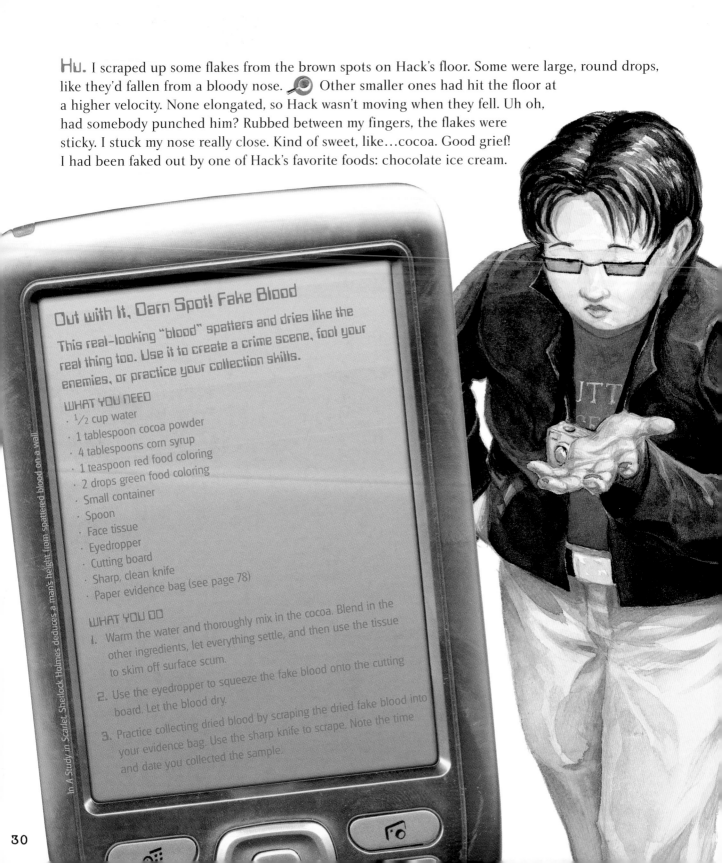 Other smaller ones had hit the floor at a higher velocity. None elongated, so Hack wasn't moving when they fell. Uh oh, had somebody punched him? Rubbed between my fingers, the flakes were sticky. I stuck my nose really close. Kind of sweet, like…cocoa. Good grief! I had been faked out by one of Hack's favorite foods: chocolate ice cream.

Out with It, Darn Spot! Fake Blood

This real-looking "blood" spatters and dries like the real thing too. Use it to create a crime scene, fool your enemies, or practice your collection skills.

WHAT YOU NEED
- 1/2 cup water
- 1 tablespoon cocoa powder
- 4 tablespoons corn syrup
- 1 teaspoon red food coloring
- 2 drops green food coloring
- Small container
- Spoon
- Face tissue
- Eyedropper
- Cutting board
- Sharp, clean knife
- Paper evidence bag (see page 78)

WHAT YOU DO
1. Warm the water and thoroughly mix in the cocoa. Blend in the other ingredients, let everything settle, and then use the tissue to skim off surface scum.
2. Use the eyedropper to squeeze the fake blood onto the cutting board. Let the blood dry.
3. Practice collecting dried blood by scraping the dried fake blood into your evidence bag. Use the sharp knife to scrape. Note the time and date you collected the sample.

My next stop was Hack's bathroom. It held some strange things: a big black umbrella and puddles of colored water in the tub. Someone had tracked colored stains on the tile floor, too, and there was a perfect footprint, made by a bare foot, right next to the tub. Was it Hack's? Or was it someone else's?

The Bare Truth: What Feet Tell Us

Did you know that you can use simple math to calculate how tall a person is by measuring his or her feet? And toe prints are as unique as fingerprints.

WHAT YOU NEED

- Friendly adult volunteer
- Measuring tape
- Notepad
- Pencil or pen
- Calculator

WHAT YOU DO

1. The length of an adult's foot is roughly 15 percent of the person's height, and this fact is useful in figuring out how tall a person is when you have only a footprint. Measure someone's foot while she's standing. Write down the measurement.

2. Let's say the person's foot is $8\frac{1}{4}$ inches long. Turn the fraction into a decimal (8.25 inches) and multiply the length of the footprint by 100. Divide that number by 15. The result is your friend's approximate height.

3. Because young people haven't stopped growing, the ratios of their body parts are different, so calculating height accurately from foot size works best with adults. But you can practice your skills with your friends.

4. Oh, and by the way, the distance from the tip of the left index finger to the tip of the right index finger, when a person's arms are raised parallel to the shoulders, is about the same as the person's height!

Homes. I spied a balled-up piece of paper on Hack's desk and uncrumpled it. Zounds! It was a handwritten letter to his folks. Odd, since Hack always typed things. This merited closer analysis. When I rescanned the words, I realized Hack had embedded a secret message, right there in the text. But it was a strange one.

> Dear Mom and Dad,
> Three guys I know are going camping. Friends of mine, so I'm going too. No problem with my homework. Time I had a little vacation. Eating is no problem because they're bringing the groceries. Will be back in a few days. Make me a sandwich in case they can't cook. You don't mind that I'm going, I hope. Sorry about the short notice.
> Hack

Hint: Read the first word of each sentence.

When I turned on the desk lamp, I spotted faint brown, scrawled marks on the lamp shade: 8 8 8 8 8. Hack must have used a fizzy soft drink to write a message there. I looked down. There, where Pink had swept up trace evidence, were shaky capital letters formed by dirt stuck to the floor: NOTMYF. One thing was clear. Hack knew his visitor, realized something was wrong, and stalled while he surreptitiously left messages for us.

Sherlock Holmes deciphers a "first word" message in the story "The Gloria Scott."

Invisible Messages

Hack wrote a message on his floor with something that would show up only when all the other dust around it was removed. See page 86 for more secret inks.

WHAT YOU NEED
- White votive candle or stub, or clear wax crayon from craft store
- Glue stick, corn syrup, or soft drink
- Paintbrush
- Baby powder
- Floor dust
- Cornstarch
- Chalk dust

WHAT YOU DO

1. Warm the candle between your hands until the wax has softened. Then use it like a pencil to write a message on a piece of paper. Or write a message with the glue stick, corn syrup, or soft drink, using the brush or your finger. Let dry.

2. Sprinkle the area with dust, baby powder, cornstarch, or chalk dust. Then gently sweep the excess away. Voilà! Message revealed.

More Invisible Messages

There are all sorts of ways to write invisible messages. This method uses heat-sensitive ink that darkens when it's warmed up.

WHAT YOU NEED
- Raw onion
- Eye protectors (optional)
- Grater
- Tea strainer
- Spoon
- Clean jar or saucer
- Brush or toothpick
- Piece of light-colored paper or cloth

WHAT YOU DO

1. Put on your eye protectors, and grate some onion into the saucer.

2. Spoon the grated onion into the tea strainer. Press the back of the spoon to the onion in the strainer, squeezing the juice out and into the jar.

3. Dip a brush or toothpick into the onion juice. Write your message on the piece of paper or cloth. Let it dry.

4. Warm the paper in a low oven or hold it close to a light bulb or radiator to reveal the message.

Homes. We had begun our investigation quietly, afraid that Hack might actually be guilty of causing the grades meltdown at school. Maybe he'd hacked into the grades as a protest. But the giant prints, strange hairs and button, and hidden, cryptic notes had no explanation. It was time to expand our search, but we agreed we should keep it quiet.

Starting the Search for a Missing Person

Here's a checklist to follow when you're looking for someone.

1. Review and evaluate the facts

   A giant intruder trashed Hack's room and Hack was gone, probably not willingly. Hack tried to leave us clues.

2. Obtain a recent photo of the missing person.

3. If you interview a witness, remember that people are notoriously unreliable. Ask your witness to describe anyone they saw: age, weight, height, clothing, hair style and color, facial hair, complexion, noticeable scars or tattoos? Listen for unsolicited information, too, and don't slant your questions.

   (That's why we won't let Pink do interviews: "So, was the suspect blonde like Suzye Sylk, or act like she smells something bad like Sylk, or look like Sylk would look in a really good disguise?")

4. What was s/he wearing when last seen?

   Hack always wore jeans and his 'I Hack, Therefore I 'Am' T-shirt. The shirt lay on the floor in his room though, so that wasn't going to help us.

5. Any tattoos, piercings, or other identifying marks?

   Nope, Hack was Mr. Average. Some of the most out-there people look entirely ordinary. They don't follow the crowd, but they don't waste energy on looking 'different,' either.

6. Has the party disappeared before, and where did s/he go?

   No, and anyone who knew Hack would laugh at the idea of him camping. He'd do it only if he had a satellite feed for his computer.

7. How did s/he disappear?

   Quite easily, if his assailant had hands the size of baked hams and was as tall as a tree.

8. Car and license plate number?

   Not applicable. He'd left behind The Malteaser Falcon.

9. Cell phone, credit cards, ATM card?

   You're kidding. His allowance was barely more than mine.

10. List of friends? Any recent conflicts or known enemies?

    Well, duh. Sylk and her gang of two hate everybody. So we'd start by focusing on them.

Pink. These are our suspects. At the top of the list, the head honcho herself, my arch-nemesis, Suzye Sylk.

Suzye Sylk is the ringleader of her gang, a total queen bee. Everyone always does what she wants. She snaps that blonde hair of hers around like a whip, and if you don't dress like her or won't do anything for her, you don't exist in her eyes. (If you ever call her by her first name, you're dead. She's Sylk. Just Sylk. Like Madonna. Or Dillinger.)  Notorious, she is naturally the number one object of my capital-S Suspicion, and I, the jury, say she's guilty! Well, I hope she's guilty. Now to prove it. Hopefully.

Penny Dreadfull is Sylk's yes-woman and me-too sidekick. I mean, look at her! Exactly the same body and clothes and bangs. Sometimes I think I detect a gleam of intelligent thought in Penny's eyes. (I caught her carrying a book once, but she claimed it was Sylk's. Hah. Not likely.) I suspect Homes likes her, but I've never gotten him to admit it. Penny never takes off her roller skates. How weird is that?

Bubbles Butler's most meaningful relationship is with his video console. I've never seen him without his video game controller. His second-most-meaningful relationship is with Sylk. She orders him around as if he were her pet poodle. He's the muscle in Sylk's gang. (Don't ask me who the brain is.) No one has ever heard Bubbles speak.

Penny

Sylk

Bubbles

The Tables Are Turned

Pink. We left Hack's house and went back to my room to review the evidence. We were most interested in the contents of Hack's trash can, though he didn't always distinguish between the can and the rest of his room. Just about anything worth knowing about a person can be revealed through a good trash cover. The inventory: balled-up Burp! Burger wrappers, candy wrappers, unsigned report card, burger wrappers, ticket stubs to the latest Fernando Bloom movie. ("That no-talent actor," Homes said.) More burger wrappers.

Trash Cover

Do you have any idea how much you can learn by going through someone's garbage? In the detecting trade, we call this a trash cover. My little brother does it to me all the time, the brat.

WHAT YOU NEED

- Full trash can (not from the kitchen or bathroom—too yucky)
- Rubber or latex gloves
- Clean white sheet or used shower curtain
- Dowel or clean wooden stick
- Tweezers
- Notepad
- Pencil
- Magnifying glass
- Sheets of white paper
- Glue stick

WHAT YOU DO

1. Nimbly convey a full trash bag and contents to your work area. Remember that, technically, trash belongs to its original owner until it's put out on the curb for pickup.

2. Wearing the gloves, spread the sheet or shower curtain on top of a flat surface.

3. Empty the trash bag's contents onto the sheet. Use the dowel and tweezers to sort the items into piles of similar things, such as papers and envelopes, containers, and miscellaneous.

4. Reassemble torn-up documents. Work on top of a clean sheet of white paper so you can glue together each masterwork when it's completed. Start by assembling the corners and edges, matching colors, patterns, letters, or handwriting. Use your magnifying glass to identify patterns, smudges and stains you can join together, and look for pieces whose ripped edges match.

5. Make a written inventory of what you find. List items under headings, such as Documents, Packaging, Clothing, Miscellaneous Objects. See any patterns?

6. If you get caught, tell people you're practicing to be an archeologist.

Pink. Suddenly, the doorbell rang. It couldn't be the mail—the postman always rings twice. There was a bundle wrapped in newsprint, "4 the deteKtives" written on top. Inside was a big, dead fish and a photo of Hack, a giant gloved hand around his neck! We all took a big sniff. This was no red herring. It was a blue mackerel. Its message: "Drop the case and butt out." Something was fishy. Homes said, "This is noteworthy. Observe the childish writing, the grade-school penmanship, and poor spelling." Trust Homes to start analyzing the handwriting before Hu and I finish reading the message.

Talk to the Hand:
Handwriting & Paper Analysis

Our handwriting is as unique as our fingerprints. The ability to analyze handwriting is essential for a gumshoe.

WHAT YOU NEED
- Ballpoint pen
- White paper
- Tracing paper
- Red, green, purple, and orange pencils
- Ruler
- Pad of ruled paper

WHAT YOU DO

1. To practice analyzing handwriting, have everyone sign his name, and then once more below it, on one sheet of paper.

2. Cover the writing with tracing paper. Make a red mark at all the high points of the writing and a green mark at the low points. Use the ruler and matching pencil to join the marks together. Are the red and green zigzag lines alike?

3. Use the orange pencil and a new sheet of tracing paper to make up-and-down strokes over the letters, following each letter's "slant." Compare the two sets of slants.

4. Compare the following items:

   • How are the i's dotted and the t's crossed?

   • How far above or below the line are the letters?

   • How are the letters connected? (Forgers learn to copy letters, but copying how they connect is much harder.)

   • How much room is at the page top and bottom?

5. Sort the samples into piles of similar writing. Compare to the signatures. Who wrote what?

Homes. We put the fish aside and stared again at the trash. Of course! Hack was trying to tell us to look in the TRASH when he stuck pinholes in the poster! Now, what was the predominant element? Burger wrappers. Why were they important?

As I looked harder at the crumpled papers, I started to laugh so hard that Pink and Hu thought I'd lost it. Whoever designed the wrapper was playing a joke. The printed symbols around the edge of the paper weren't just decoration. They were actually the famous Pigpen Cipher, used since the 1700s.  All the way around the edge of the wrapper, the cipher read:

EAT BADD BUY BADD PLAY BADD EAT BADD BUY BADD PLAY BADD

But why would someone go to so much trouble to put a cipher on the wrappers?

Hint: Compare the wrapper designs to the cipher at right.

In "The Dancing Men," Holmes claims to have analyzed 160 different ciphers.

Pigpen Cipher

This is how to figure out the pigpen cipher. Use it for your own secret messages. This cipher has also been called the Masonic cipher and the Free Mason's cipher.

WHAT YOU NEED
- Pencil
- Paper
- Secret message

WHAT YOU DO
1. Draw two tic-tac-toe grids and two big Xs from left to right on the paper.
2. In the second grid, put a dot in each cell, near the lines.
3. In the second X, put a dot in each of the four sections, near where the lines cross.
4. Starting with the first tic-tac-toe grid, write an A in the top left-hand corner.
5. Moving from left to right, fill the tic-tac-toe box with the first nine letters of the alphabet. Repeat this in the next box with the next nine letters.
6. In the first X, write an S in the top V. Fill in the rest of the letters, moving from left to right and then putting the last letter in the bottom V. Repeat this on the second X to complete the alphabet.
7. Use each shape to represent that letter when coding your secret message.

40

Hu. Something about that burger wrapper cipher was bugging me. It felt familiar, but I didn't know why. All those Bs, As, Ds, Bs, over and over… I ran over to Pink's computer, which was running that BaddBoyz screen saver Burp! Burgers kept handing out. A stream of colored dingbats looped across the screen, repeating with exactly the same rhythm as the Pigpen message!

The screen saver was a coded message—and I was pretty sure it said the same thing the Burp! Burger wrappers did because the symbols repeated the same way.

I looked closer. Something looked strange about the As in the message. I zoomed in on the tiny space inside the flower. *Aaargh!* The grinning face of Burp the Clown, the Burp! Burgers' mascot, appeared. The circus music on Hack's computer was starting to make sense. BaddBoyz and Burp! Burgers must be in this together, whatever *this* was.

Cracking Codes

Most of the codes people use are substitution codes, which means each letter in the message is replaced by one other symbol, letter, or number. These codes are fairly easy to break.

WHAT YOU NEED

- Photocopier (optional)
- Pencil
- Paper

WHAT YOU DO

1. If you can, photocopy the code. If you don't have a photocopier, copy the code onto another piece of paper. Leave a blank line between each line of the message.

2. Figure out one symbol at a time. When you think you know what letter a symbol represents, write it down above the symbol. Go through the entire message, writing the letter above the symbol each time it appears.

3. The easiest symbols to figure out are A and I. These are the only letters that will appear by themselves.

4. Look for symbols that appear twice in a row. This will usually indicates a double letter. Try using OO, EE, PP, LL, TT, DD, SS, MM, or NN where you think a double letter may be.

5. Are there symbols in your code that you keep seeing over and over again? These could be the letters E, H, S, or T—the four most common letters used in English words.

41

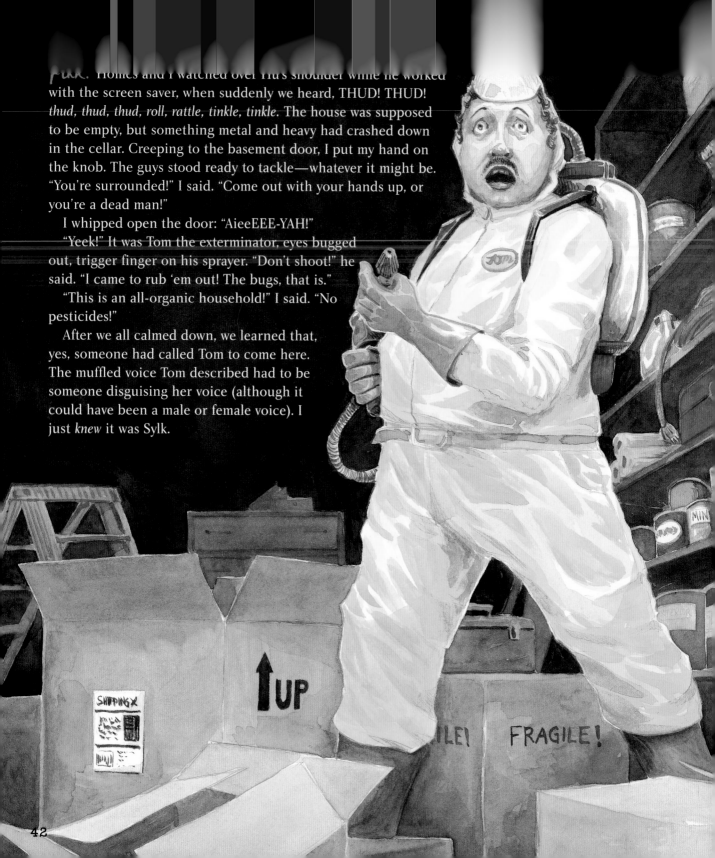

...Holmes and I watched over Hu's shoulder while he worked with the screen saver, when suddenly we heard, THUD! THUD! *thud, thud, thud, roll, rattle, tinkle, tinkle.* The house was supposed to be empty, but something metal and heavy had crashed down in the cellar. Creeping to the basement door, I put my hand on the knob. The guys stood ready to tackle—whatever it might be. "You're surrounded!" I said. "Come out with your hands up, or you're a dead man!"

I whipped open the door: "AieeEEE-YAH!"

"Yeek!" It was Tom the exterminator, eyes bugged out, trigger finger on his sprayer. "Don't shoot!" he said. "I came to rub 'em out! The bugs, that is."

"This is an all-organic household!" I said. "No pesticides!"

After we all calmed down, we learned that, yes, someone had called Tom to come here. The muffled voice Tom described had to be someone disguising her voice (although it could have been a male or female voice). I just *knew* it was Sylk.

Disguising Your Voice

Sometimes it's useful to know how to disguise your voice, and, no, I don't mean so you can make prank phone calls.

WHAT YOU NEED

- Clothespin
- Washcloth or handkerchief
- TV or radio
- Comb and brush with wire bristles
- Wax paper
- Kazoo, available in music stores
- Brand-new unsharpened pencil
- Raw onion
- Paring knife
- Slice of bread with peanut butter spread on it
- Voice-altering computer software (talk to a parent about this)

WHAT YOU DO

1. Pinch your nose closed. You can keep it closed with the clothespin (ow). Talk.

2. Cover the telephone receiver with a cloth, and have TV or radio noise in the background to muffle your voice. Create "static" by scratching the comb through the brush or crinkling wax paper near the receiver.

3. Put the kazoo in your mouth and sing into it; you won't believe what it does to your voice. If you're a guy, tap your Adam's apple while talking.

4. Clench the pencil crossways in your teeth as you speak.

5. Carefully slice the onion, holding it close enough to start the waterworks in your nose and eyes. Cram your mouth with the bread and peanut butter. Guaranteed to gunk up your diction!

6. If you talk to people via the Internet on your computer, download free software that morphs the sound of your voice. Get a parent's permission for this.

Homes. It was time to split up. Hu would research connections between BaddBoyz and Burp! Burgers. Pink would tail Sylk and Penny. And I had the task of searching Penny's and Bubbles' rooms. It seemed simple enough—but caution is always the better part of valor. I'd have to be careful to make sure no one snooped on me while I was snooping on them. One advantage of having a cleaner room than mine: it's much easier to know if someone's searched your room while you were out. On the other hand, my brain can overcome any obstacle. I quickly booby-trapped my room.

Stop Thief! Powder and Other Best Booby Traps

There are several ways to booby-trap a room, in case you need evidence that your kid sister is messing with your stuff.

WHAT YOU NEED
- Fluorescent detection powder* or talcum powder
- Paintbrush
- Lamp
- Black lightbulb
- Hair
- Thread
- Toothpick
- Paper clip

*Available on the Internet at detective sites.

WHAT YOU DO
1. Brush the fluorescent powder on important items. Don't use powder on electronic equipment or other things that could be damaged by it. To check if someone's touched the powder, screw the black lightbulb into the lamp and turn off any other lights. Viewing the items under the black light, you'll see marks if someone's touched the powder. Also, examine suspects' fingers in the dark, under the black light. Glowing? Guilty! (You can use talcum powder for this instead, but it won't glow in the dark.)

2. Use spit to stick a hair or thread over the seams of windows or doors. If it's not there when you get back, someone has been in your room.

3. Jam the toothpick or paper clip in a drawer or door as you close it. If it's on the floor later, you'll know someone opened it.

4. Make notes of exact positions of furniture, clothing, books, etc. Check if they've been moved while you were out.

The Drawer Trap

A single piece of tape is a sticky solution for stopping sneaks.

WHAT YOU NEED
- Drawer
- Clear tape

WHAT YOU DO
1. Open the drawer below the one you want to put the alarm on.

2. Tear off a small piece of tape about $1\frac{1}{2}$ inches long.

3. Stick one end of the tape to the underside of the drawer you're putting the alarm on. Stick the other end to the frame.

4. If anyone opens the drawer, the end of the tape on the frame will detach and stick to the bottom of the drawer.

5. To check whether the drawer has been opened, open the drawer below and look up at the bottom of the drawer you put the alarm on.

6. Remember, if you open the drawer you put the tape on before checking it from beneath, you won't be able to tell whether you set off the alarm or someone else did.

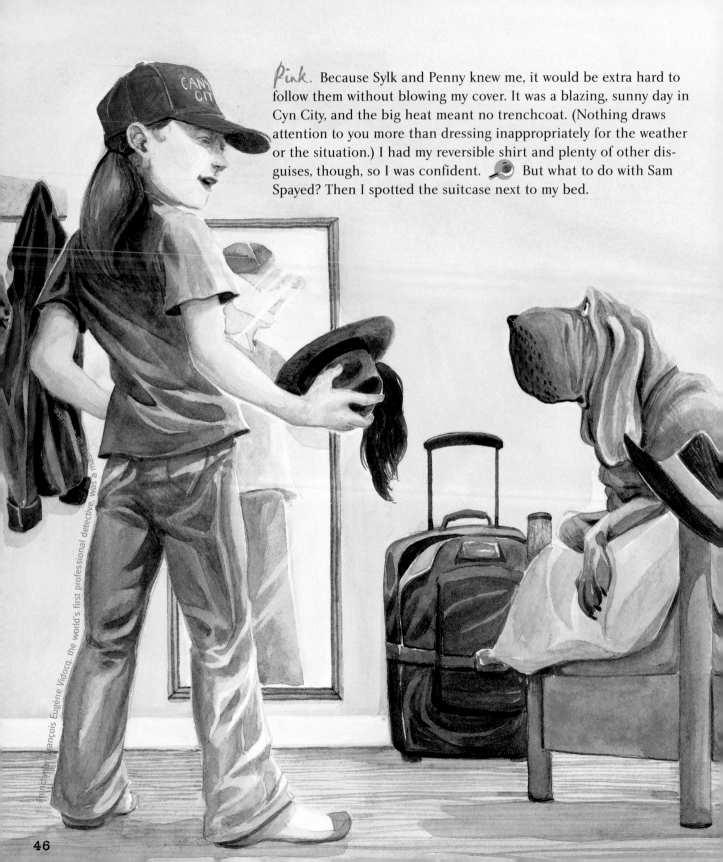

Pink. Because Sylk and Penny knew me, it would be extra hard to follow them without blowing my cover. It was a blazing, sunny day in Cyn City, and the big heat meant no trenchcoat. (Nothing draws attention to you more than dressing inappropriately for the weather or the situation.) I had my reversible shirt and plenty of other disguises, though, so I was confident. But what to do with Sam Spayed? Then I spotted the suitcase next to my bed.

Other Disguises

Don't forget to change your face and hair while you're changing your shirt!

WHAT YOU NEED

- Hair gel
- Fake ponytail, available in costume stores
- Velcro tape
- Scissors
- Baseball cap
- Cotton pads or big pack of bubble gum
- Sunglasses and regular glasses with lenses removed
- Roll of gauze bandaging
- Handkerchief
- Spare change
- Shoes with laces
- Glue

WHAT YOU DO

1. Wear your hair up, down, parted differently, or gelled. Use the velcro tape to attach the ponytail to the baseball cap; then hide your own hair up in the cap.

2. Give yourself chipmunk cheeks by packing them with cotton or bubble gum.

3. Switch between sunglasses, eyeglasses, and no glasses. Wrap thick layers of gauze over the ends of the temple pieces of one pair of glasses and glue in place. They'll make your ears stick out.

4. If you need to hide your face, pretend to search in your backpack or blow your nose with the handkerchief. Drop some change and bend to pick it up, or retie your shoelaces.

5. Change your posture and walk differently. Hunch over and lower your head. Shuffle instead of striding.

Reversible Shirt

A good private dick needs to be a quick-change artist, slipping in and out of disguises while blending in with the crowd. It helps to have a T-shirt like this one.

WHAT YOU NEED

- 2 T-shirts: same size, different colors
- Fabric glue

WHAT YOU DO

1. Turn one shirt inside out. Put it inside the other shirt, matching the necklines, hemlines, armholes, and sleeve edges.

2. Apply the glue to the side seams, neck and sleeve edges, and hems between the two shirt layers.

3. Press together and let dry.

4. You can do the same thing with thin jackets, scarves, and even pants! Have fun and experiment. Double coats will make you look bigger and heavier, too.

Chapter 4

The Chase Is On

Pink. I was on Sylk and Penny like a cheap suit, and naturally they went to the mall. Those two never stopped shopping or worrying about their hair. Blech. But duty called, and I used my best sneaking tactics to keep an eye on them. Because the mall frowned on dogs, I stuffed Sam in my wheeled suitcase and dragged him behind me. (Note to self: Put Sam on a diet.) I brought my hidden camera (see page 15), too, in case the girls did something interesting.

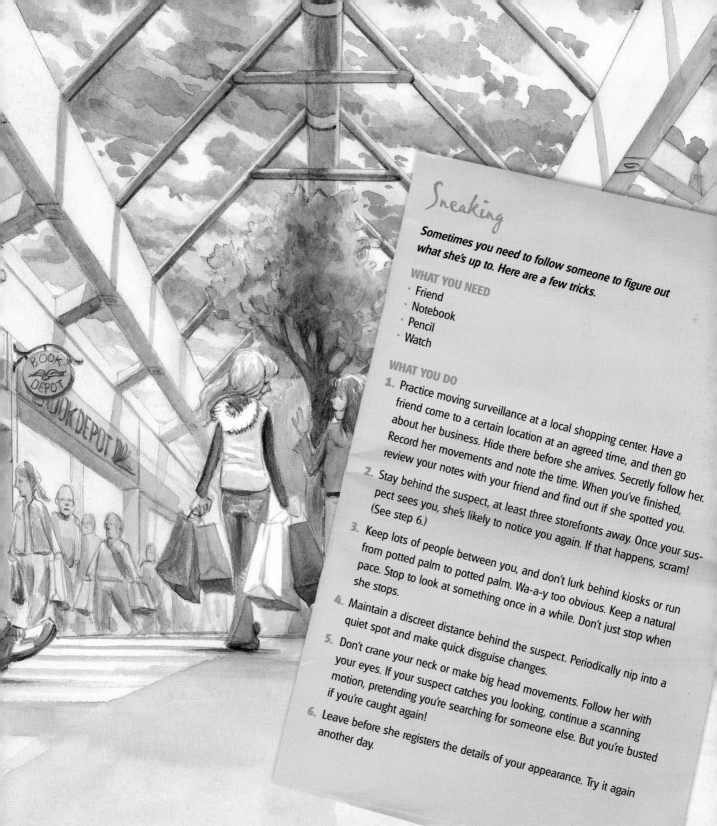

Sneaking

Sometimes you need to follow someone to figure out what she's up to. Here are a few tricks.

WHAT YOU NEED

- Friend
- Notebook
- Pencil
- Watch

WHAT YOU DO

1. Practice moving surveillance at a local shopping center. Have a friend come to a certain location at an agreed time, and then go about her business. Hide there before she arrives. Secretly follow her. Record her movements and note the time. When you've finished, review your notes with your friend and find out if she spotted you.

2. Stay behind the suspect, at least three storefronts away. Once your suspect sees you, she's likely to notice you again. If that happens, scram! (See step 6.)

3. Keep lots of people between you, and don't lurk behind kiosks or run from potted palm to potted palm. Wa-a-y too obvious. Keep a natural pace. Stop to look at something once in a while. Don't just stop when she stops.

4. Maintain a discreet distance behind the suspect. Periodically nip into a quiet spot and make quick disguise changes.

5. Don't crane your neck or make big head movements. Follow her with your eyes. If your suspect catches you looking, continue a scanning motion, pretending you're searching for someone else. But you're busted if you're caught again!

6. Leave before she registers the details of your appearance. Try it again another day.

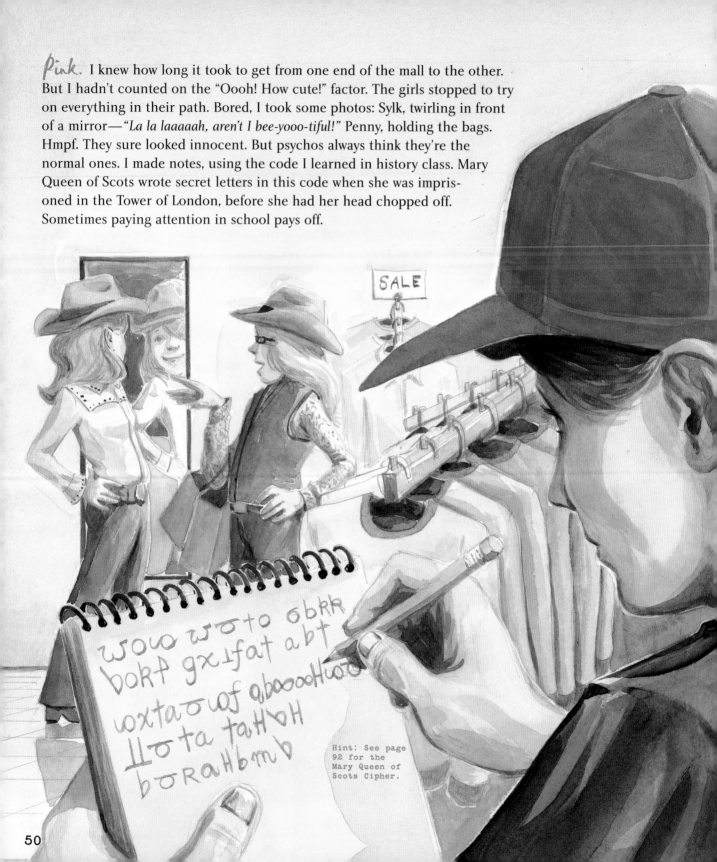

Pink. I knew how long it took to get from one end of the mall to the other. But I hadn't counted on the "Oooh! How cute!" factor. The girls stopped to try on everything in their path. Bored, I took some photos: Sylk, twirling in front of a mirror—*"La la laaaaah, aren't I bee-yooo-tiful!"* Penny, holding the bags. Hmpf. They sure looked innocent. But psychos always think they're the normal ones. I made notes, using the code I learned in history class. Mary Queen of Scots wrote secret letters in this code when she was imprisoned in the Tower of London, before she had her head chopped off. Sometimes paying attention in school pays off.

SALE

Hint: See page 92 for the Mary Queen of Scots Cipher.

Time Is of the Essence

It's important to know how long it takes to get from point A to point B when you're tailing a suspect.

WHAT YOU NEED
- Group of friends
- Stopwatch
- Notepad
- Pencil

WHAT YOU DO

1. Working with your friends, measure how long it takes for each of you to travel between important landmarks in your neighborhood: house to mailbox, front door to backyard, completely around your house, from your house to your best friend's house, etc. Use the stopwatch to measure the times as you walk, jog, and run.

2. Now you can estimate how long it takes a suspect to travel a certain path. Let's say that your suspect claims she left point A and walked briskly to point B. You know that she should arrive at point B about six minutes after she was seen at point A. Does she? (And if she arrives ten minutes later than she should have, what transpired during that time?)

In "The Empty House," Holmes uses a wax dummy the same way to fool his archenemy, Colonel Moran.

Homes. Before I left on my mission, I prepared a little something to confuse my enemies. I put a silhouette in the window of my bedroom. Anyone watching my house while I searched Penny and Bubbles' rooms would think I was at home. 🔍

Faking It: Making a Cut-Out Silhouette

Make more than one and it will look as if you're having a party in your room.

WHAT YOU NEED
- Chair
- A friend
- Masking tape
- Large piece of cardboard plus scrap cardboard
- Lamp
- Marker or pencil
- Scissors
- Books or shoes

WHAT YOU DO

1. Sit in the chair, facing parallel to a wall. Have a friend tape the cardboard on the wall about waist height.

2. Turn off the overhead light. Have your friend position the unshaded lamp to cast your life-sized shadow onto the cardboard.

3. Have your friend trace your profile on the cardboard.

4. Cut out the profile. Use the books or shoes to prop it in front of a window, or cut out a triangular piece of cardboard and jam it into a slit in the bottom of the profile to make a "stand."

Hu. I was on my way home, thinking about the case and a big bowl of chocolate ice cream (I don't care what Homes says about vegetables—ice cream is the perfect brain food!) when—*Rustle, Rustle*. Someone was behind me! Suddenly I felt very solo, in a lonely place. Be cool, Hu. I shifted into ultra-evasion mode to shake my tail.

Mean Streets: Shaking a Tail

Don't lead someone to your destination when you're being followed.

WHAT YOU NEED
· Your wits
· Every opportunity around you

WHAT TO DO
1. Never look directly at the goon 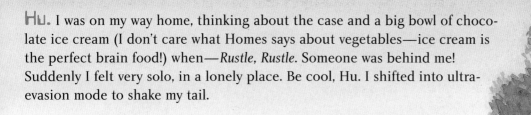 following you. You don't want him to know that you know he's there.

2. While a group of people or a car blocks you from his sight, change direction or slip down a side street.

3. Casually walk in a store and then out a back exit. Or, hide in a bathroom or dressing room until the coast is clear.

4. Duck down an alley and change disguises. Leave the way you came.

5. Go where you never meant to be in the first place. Pretend to collect a secret message. The goon will think he's discovered your true destination and stop following you. (For fun, return the next day and leave a coded message full of false information in the same spot. The goon will collect it and think he's intercepted a real message.)

Homes. I was careful to look for booby traps in Penny's room. I suspected she was the brightest of the three, despite those ridiculous roller skates. Penny was good at hiding things, but I was better. But—the HORROR! Penny had a huge crush on that wretched movie star Fernando Bloom! There were notes to him and pictures hidden away everywhere.

I unrolled a poster to find it plastered with a big, fat, lipstick kiss. Yuck.

When I checked under the false bottom of a jewelry box, a magazine photo of Bloom grinned up at me.

I peeled away the lining of a shoe to find a coded note. I decoded it, then made a mental note for later: Throw up. Violently.

So far, it was the Lost Weekend. Penny had nothing incriminating (other than evidence of her poor taste in crush material) hidden in her room. On I went to Bubbles' house.

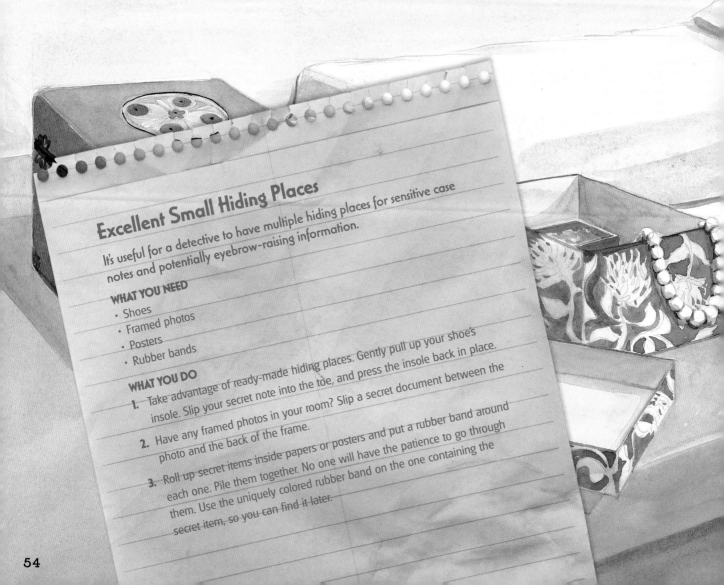

Excellent Small Hiding Places

It's useful for a detective to have multiple hiding places for sensitive case notes and potentially eyebrow-raising information.

WHAT YOU NEED
- Shoes
- Framed photos
- Posters
- Rubber bands

WHAT YOU DO
1. Take advantage of ready-made hiding places. Gently pull up your shoe's insole. Slip your secret note into the toe, and press the insole back in place.
2. Have any framed photos in your room? Slip a secret document between the photo and the back of the frame.
3. Roll up secret items inside papers or posters and put a rubber band around each one. Pile them together. No one will have the patience to go through them. Use the uniquely colored rubber band on the one containing the secret item, so you can find it later.

Hint: Write the code backward and take out the Xs.

False-Bottom Box

This trick is simple and discreet—that's why it's a classic hiding place.

WHAT YOU NEED
- Shoebox
- Cardboard
- Pencil
- Scissors
- Gift wrap
- Glue

WHAT YOU DO

1. Put the shoebox on top of the cardboard. Outline its base with the pencil.

2. Cut out the shape, just inside the lines. Glue gift wrap to the cutout. When the glue is dry, put your secret item in the box and gently press the false bottom in place.

3. Adapt this technique to make false drawer bottoms covered with shelf paper on top of the item.

Homes. Bubbles' room was about what I'd expected. No books, no art, no musical instruments. Just a set of barbells, video games, games, games, and piles of gaming magazines. The BaddBoyz logo screen saver flickered on the computer monitor, and a top-of-the-line gaming system whirred in the corner, ready for instant action.

I reached under the mattress and drew out a fistful of games. They were Hack's! Bless Bubbles and his total lack of imagination. He'd have done better hiding them among his own games.  I might not have found them then.

Then it hit me. There was something much larger going on here than the Pink Pinkerton Detective Agency had assumed. All the clues had been there from the very beginning. Methodically, I started to take Bubbles' room apart, looking for the evidence to support my theory.

Excellent Large Hiding Places

There are tons of potential hiding places in your home, especially if you're willing to do some of your own cleaning.

WHAT YOU NEED

- Paper envelopes
- Pieces of cardboard in mixed sizes
- Re-sealable plastic bags
- Masking tape
- Scissors
- Safety pins

WHAT YOU DO

1. Survey your house. Look for chairs with zippered cushions, pillows with zippered cases, or shams. Seal your secret documents in envelopes and slip them inside the cushion covers, on the under-side or facing the back. The box springs under a mattress frequently have small rips on the bottom, so you can slip something inside. (Don't put anything directly under a mattress—that's the first place anybody will think to look.)

2. Trim pieces of cardboard so you can wedge them up under chair seats, between the legs. Tape flat items to the "hidden" side before wedging.

3. Tape things to drawer bottoms, under tabletops, and behind pictures or mirrors with masking tape.

4. Silk flower arrangements stuck in floral foam are great for stashing stuff. Loosen the foam and gen-tly lift the whole arrangement from the container. Put your item in the container and replace the arrangement.

5. If you have a dog, stick things under his bed. He won't tell. Or seal items in a plastic bag and slip it under the cat litter box. (This means you have to clean the box yourself every day—but no one will ever find what you hid.)

6. Hide stuff in the bottom of your laundry hamper. (Again, you'll have to do your own laundry.) Slide things inside folded clothing and put them at the bottom of drawers or piles in the closet.

7. Pin envelopes of secret stuff on the hidden side of your window curtains. Tape flat documents to the underside of lamps.

Homes. I was supposed to send a message if I found anything suspicious in any one of the evil trio's rooms. Time for our secret color code! So I ran to Ratner's Deli and had a platter of canapés  delivered to Hu's house. There's more than one way of embedding a secret message!

This fancy finger food is frequently served to guests in drawing-room mysteries right before somebody gets bumped off.

Hint: Read the toothpick
colors from left to right.

yellow	SYLK
purple	PENNY
blue	BUBBLES
orange	URGENT
green	FIND
black	HIDE
white	LUNCH?

Color Codes and Secret Drops

Color codes are amazing and incredibly versatile. You can pass messages right in front of other people without anyone realizing what's going on and anything can be your message.

WHAT YOU NEED

- A friend
- Paper
- Pencil
- Newspaper
- Milk jug caps
- Craft paints
- Paintbrush

WHAT YOU DO

1. With a friend, list the words you want to use in your code. Assign a color to each word or phrase. Memorize the code and destroy the list. If you have more words than colors, try the Complex Color Codes.

2. Spread out the newspaper and paint pairs of caps the same color: 2 red, 2 yellow, etc. Paint a pair of caps for each word in your code.

3. Let the paint dry. Then divide the caps into two sets. Give one set to your friend and keep one for yourself.

4. Agree on places to hide the messages, maybe under rocks, plant pots, yard furniture, or parked bicycles.

5. When you have a message to send to your friend, use the colored caps to compose the message. Go to the place you agreed on in step 4 and carefully hide the bottle caps there. Make sure you aren't being observed.

Complex Color Codes

You can make your color code even more complex by assigning multiple meanings to the same color. This will make it harder for someone else to break your code!

WHAT YOU NEED

- A friend
- Pencil
- Paper
- Colorful items

WHAT YOU DO

1. Make a list of words and phrases you want to use in your code.

2. Assign each word a color and a placement. For example, a red bandanna in your left pocket might mean, "We're being watched," while a red bandanna in your right pocket could mean, "Meet me behind the gym after school."

3. Memorize the code and destroy your list.

4. How many more ways can you think of to convey color codes? Try clothing, jewelry, socks, toothbrushes, toothpicks, colored pencils, or even soda straws. Or make a snack of raw veggies and try Homes' method.

Hu. I was still staring at the screen, then—what the heck? A canapé platter from Homes? Festive. But then I decoded the toothpicks. Bubbles! BaddBoyz! Burp! Burgers! The case was starting to break.

I text-messaged Pink's cell phone, using Homes' favorite cipher.

8 100 100 19 # 8
9 9 8 9 9 # 4 #
84 15 84 84 82
100 29 # 84 18 8
8 # 18 21 8 # 84
15 51 19 # 29 18
7 100 # 18 8 8
51 100 29 29 #
777 # 7 18 51 82
9 39 100 # 8 51

IN THE YEAR 1878 I took my degree of Doctor of Medicine of the University of London, and proceeded to Netley to go through the course prescribed for surgeons in the Army. Having completed my studies there, I was duly attached to the Fifth Northumberland Fusiliers as assistant surgeon. The regiment was stationed in India at the time, and before I could join it, the second Afghan war had broken out. On landing at Bombay, I learned that my corps had advanced through the passes, and was already deep in the enemy's country. I followed, however, with many other officers who were in the same situation as myself, and succeeded in reaching Candahar in safety, where I found my regiment, and at once entered upon my new duties.

Hint: Use this page to decode the cell phone message. See step 1 of the instructions on the next page.

A Study in Scarlet was the first story about Sherlock Holmes

Send   Attach   Addresses   Fonts   Color

To: pink@pinkpinkertonagency.com

CC: sherman@pinkpinkertonagency.com

Subject: Project

Book Cipher

Book ciphers are good for us literary detectives. You can also use a favorite short story or a dictionary. Just be sure you and your colleagues use the same edition so there's no confusion.

WHAT YOU NEED

- 2 identical books (not from the library!)
- Pencil

WHAT YOU DO

1. Beginning with the first word on page 1 of your texts, start numbering each word.

2. When you write your messages, the number 1 will be the code for the first letter of the first word. Number 2 will be the code for the first letter of the second word. And so on.

Pink. Sam was snoring in the suitcase and I was half-stupefied—still tailing the two dimwits at the mall—when my cell phone vibrated. No sooner had I decoded Hu's message than I was streaking back home to change clothes. Finally, some action! It was getting dark, but it was time for me to pay a visit to *777 Marlowe Drive*.

I wasn't sure when I'd get back from my little outing, so I took pains to leave myself all safe and asleep in my bed. What parents don't know can't hurt them, right? But I knew I'd be s-o-o-o grounded if I got caught.

Being There (Not): How to Make a Fake Body

Sometimes you need to make a fake body so that anybody who might look into your room will see you sleeping soundly—even if you're not there.

WHAT YOU NEED

- Pair of pajamas
- Bath or beach towels, at least 4
- Assortment of soft pillows
- Balloon that matches your skin color (or at least comes close)
- 2 latex gloves
- Pair of socks
- Roll of toilet paper

WHAT YOU DO

1. Pull down the covers and stretch the pajamas flat on the bed. Roll up the towels and stuff them in the arms and legs of the pajamas.

2. Stick pillows inside the chest area of the pajama top and in the hips of the pajama pants. Smush them into place.

3. Blow up the balloon until it's about the size of your head and tie it closed. Stuff the gloves and socks with toilet paper.

4. Carefully turn the headless pajama body on its side so it faces away from the door. Cross the top leg over the other, bending both a little at the knees. Put the stuffed socks where the feet should be.

5. Position the body's shoulders against the edge of your bed pillow and stick the lower arm under the pillow. Add a stuffed "hand" to the arm.

6. Position the balloon head on the pillow and put another pillow over it, to make it look like you're covering your head to block out light and sound. Lift the top arm, sticking part of it and the glove "hand" under the top pillow.

7. Cover the fake body with the sheets and blankets, but not too neatly! Lights out.

Night Surveillance Outfit

Turning yourself into a moving, shaggy fuzzball will help you blend into the scenery. And if you're sneaking up on someone, don't forget to wear your sneakers.  (Why do you think they're called sneakers?)

WHAT YOU NEED

- Lots of assorted pieces of dark fabric
- Scissors
- Fabric glue
- Old shirt and pants in dark colors
- Dark watch cap or baseball cap
- Sneakers
- Old pair of dark socks
- Dark gloves (optional)

WHAT YOU DO

1. Find which direction is easiest to rip the fabric. Make little cuts along one end of the fabric, about 2 inches apart. Now rip the fabric into strips. Cut the strips into different lengths, from 4 to 6 inches long. They don't have to be regular—in fact, they'll work better if they're not.

2. Apply glue to one end of each fabric strip. Starting at the shirt's hem edge and the cuffs, place the strips irregularly, sticking them to the shirt and overlapping them. Most of each strip should remain free and unglued. Apply the strips generously, covering the entire shirt. Put extras at the neck and wrists to help disguise where the suit stops and you start.

3. Repeat step 2 with the pants and the cap. Let the glue dry overnight.

4. Ready to go out? Put on the suit and cap. If your sneakers are light-colored, slip the socks over them, and then cut away part of the sock at the soles to give you better traction. Pull on the gloves.

5. You're all set. If you're on surveillance and hear someone coming, just crouch down into a ball and be still. You'll look like a shrub!

6. This outfit is dark for nighttime use. If you want, make a "daytime" version in lighter-colored fabrics.

Pink. It was a dark and stormy night. Well, dark anyway.

I crept toward the Marlowe Drive warehouse, staying in the shadows. Voices! So I hopped behind a parked delivery van. There was a huge sign of Burp the Clown on the van, holding out a big, juicy burger and saying "HAVE MORE!" The H, M, O, and E glowed in the dark. Hack had been here! He always had his glow tape on him because he did so much computer work in the dark. Hack marked important things (like the light switch) with it.

He'd left a message here: HMOE. Hmoe? H. Moe? Who was that? Perhaps Homes and Hu would know.

Night Work: Stuff That Glows in the Dark

A detective frequently operates in conditions of darkness and sometimes needs to move fast. Here's how to prepare your equipment and practice for nighttime detection.

WHAT YOU NEED

- Glow-in-the-dark adhesive tape
- Scissors
- Glow-in-the-dark stickers
- Black permanent marker
- Glow sticks
- Large piece of dark fabric
- Detecting kit
- Camera

WHAT YOU DO

1. Cut short pieces of glow-in-the-dark tape to wrap around the handle of your flashlight. Wrap tape around the handle of your detecting kit and mark the kit's four corners with four more pieces of tape so you won't stumble over it in the dark.

2. Put stickers on the corners of your camera and the lids of the storage boxes and jars in your kit. Write the box contents on each sticker.

3. To examine something in the dark without anyone seeing you, crouch down, throw the fabric over your head and shoulders, and break the glow stick. The light will illuminate whatever you're examining. Wrap the stick in the fabric when you're finished.

4. Practice moving undetected in the dark. Gently attach the stickers to large pieces of furniture and the corners of your room. Mark the desk edges, the top of a bookcase, and the bed, for example. Turn off the lights and move around silently, using the stickers to get your bearings. Now remove the stickers and see if you can do it again without running into anything.

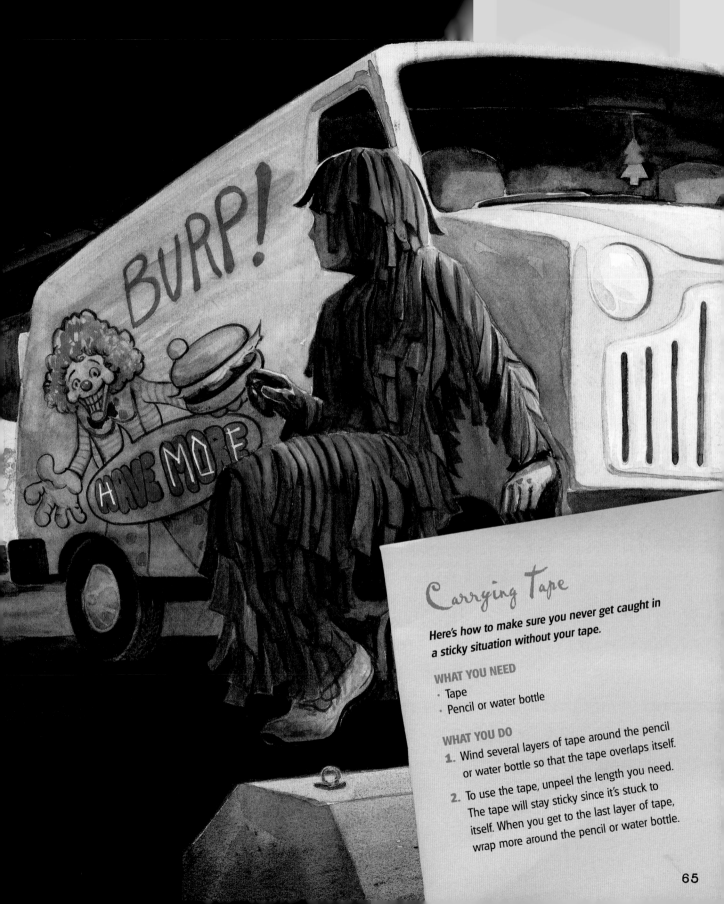

Carrying Tape

Here's how to make sure you never get caught in a sticky situation without your tape.

WHAT YOU NEED
- Tape
- Pencil or water bottle

WHAT YOU DO
1. Wind several layers of tape around the pencil or water bottle so that the tape overlaps itself.
2. To use the tape, unpeel the length you need. The tape will stay sticky since it's stuck to itself. When you get to the last layer of tape, wrap more around the pencil or water bottle.

Pink. But then I caught a glimpse of workers in biohazard suits in the warehouse window. I crept closer. They clustered around a moving assembly line carrying hundreds of bright squares of—something.

Oh. My. Gosh. The squares were Burp! Burgers' burger wrappers. A suit with a big silver tank walked up, lifted a hose and blasted the wrappers with a fine spray. The light caught the tank. It read: NANOTECH.

They were infecting the wrappers with tiny nanotech machines, small enough to be…eaten. Which meant every Burp! burger had something in it. And it was Badd.

I dialed Hu and started tapping a single key: -... .- -.. -.. / . -. .-.. / -... .- / -... .- -. . --- / .-- . .-.. --- /
- --- / .-- . --- .. ... --- -. / -... .- -. . -. -. .. .- ... / -.-. .-. . .-.. .-.. / .-- . --- .-.. .. -.-. .

Coded Morse Message

You can practice your Morse skills with a friend using light and sound.

WHAT YOU NEED
- A friend
- Flashlight, room light, or table light
- Wall, pipe, or anything tappable
- Paper
- Pencil

WHAT TO DO
1. Flick the flashlight or light switch on and off while your friend follows the Morse alphabet below and decodes the message, writing it down. One long flash equals a long dash; two short flashes equal a dot in Morse.

2. Stand on opposite sides of a wall and "knock" the message. Two knocks equal a dot, and four knocks equal a dash.

A	.-	J	.---	S	...
B	-...	K	-.-	T	-
C	-.-.	L	.-..	U	..-
D	-..	M	--	V	...-
E	.	N	-.	W	.--
F	..-.	O	---	X	-..-
G	--.	P	.--.	Y	-.--
H	....	Q	--.-	Z	--..
I	..	R	.-.		

When I heard sirens in the distance, I slipped away. I couldn't stop to ans
a million questions. Time to regroup with Homes and Hu.

Chapter 5

Closing In

Homes. Back at agency headquarters, we reviewed the facts. The BBBBB warehouse operation was busted, but Hack and Bubbles were still missing. Bubbles had all of Hack's games. Bubbles was the likely kidnapper. And I thought I knew why.

"But what about the giant prints?" Hu asked. "It's Bigfoot!"

"No, no, no!" Pink protested. "It's Sylk! She's so awful, it has to be her!"

I knew they were wrong.

"There's not a shred of evidence to connect Sylk," I said. "And mythical creatures? No. Consider the two notes. The misspelling of DeteKtiveS? Hack's goodbye note didn't mean he was SoRe, as in pain or angry. Hack's a better speller than that! Think about what he's got hanging on the wall of his room. The note was supposed to be saying he was SORRY."

"And," I continued, "Bigfoot's a myth! If you review what we know about prints, it's been obvious all along that Hack's attacker was normal-sized."

Once we reviewed all the facts we thought it was worthwhile to check Bubbles' house again.

Edgar Allan Poe invented this word for the process of logical analysis.

Elementary, My Dear

A logical mind is a detective's best ally. Here are the simple rules of ratiocination.

WHAT YOU NEED

- A brain
- Paper
- Pencil
- This book

WHAT YOU DO

1. First, let's get one thing straight. Sherlock Holmes is famous for his powers of deduction, right? Wrong. Actually, he uses two ways of thinking, called deduction and induction, and he uses induction more.

2. Induction is when you reason backward, from the particular to the general, from specific events and facts to a likely root cause. Working objectively, you find an overarching explanation for all those facts. The key is not to be influenced by what you want or wish. Otherwise, you may twist the facts to fit a theory. (Paying attention, Pink?)

3. Deduction is reasoning from the general to the particular. You come up with a master theory and then think about what it implies, all the things that can follow logically from it.

4. Now, think logically and review the story:

1. What are all the known facts and events?

   Vaporized grades, missing Hack, infectious nanotech on burger wrappers, for a start. What else?

2. What's present and what's missing at the scene of the crime? (Here's a gimme: There are only empty game cases in Hack's room. See page 16.)

3. Unique or unusual evidence can be one of your best clues:

   How big are the prints in Hack's room? (See page 22.)

4. Pay attention to details:

   How do we know the intruder is normal size? (See pages 22 and 31.)

5. Gather all the relevant evidence:

   What did Pink find on Hack's pillow? (See page 25.)

6. Perform experiments to gather fresh information.

   Go measure the buttons on your clothes. That's all I'm saying.

7. Review all the evidence in light of what you know about the crime, and create a hypothesis.

   (I think I know why Bubbles kidnapped Hack. What are Bubbles' most noticeable characteristics? (See pages 35 and 56.)

As Holmes said, "When you have excluded the impossible, whatever remains, however improbable, must be the truth."

Pink. Sure enough, Bubbles was playing video games when we arrived at his house. But Bubbles was dressed in full clown costume, just like Burp!

We surrounded him so he couldn't get away. I crossed my fingers behind my back and used my best questioning techniques:

"Sylk told me she likes you in that clown outfit. When did she help you pick it out?" Silence.

"We know you took Hack. Is he hidden at the warehouse or here?" Silence.

"Talk!" (Fingers crossed.) "Or I'll smash your game collection!"

Silence. But Bubbles' eyes teared up. I felt bad.

Then I had a brainwave. H. Moe wasn't a person, Hack left code for HOME. Bubbles had taken Hack back to Hack's own house!

We took off for Hack's, bringing Bubbles with us.

telling what you know. Also known as spilling the beans.

Getting Bubbles to Bubble

There are plenty of ways to trick a suspect into bubbling.

WHAT YOU NEED
- Willing friend

WHAT YOU DO

1. Real criminal investigators rely on their knowledge of human behavior and their wits to get people to talk, not brute force. You need to get them to like you and then steer the conversation.

2. Make small talk to establish a relationship with the suspect. Talk about things he likes, then transition to asking questions.

3. Never ask questions he can answer with a simple "Yes" or "No." Start with questions of fact. ("Homes, you and Penny have the same lunch period. Where do you sit relative to each other?")

4. Assess the person's personality. What motivates him? Adjust your questions accordingly so he identifies with you. ("I totally agree with you that dumb girls are boring. What told you that Penny's smart?")

5. Pretend you know more than you do. ("I saw you looking at Penny in class the other day. I'm sure she likes you.")

6. Keep the ball rolling. Let the conversation wander a bit, then refocus it. Take notes only if it won't distract the suspect. Repeat questions, phrasing them differently.

7. Watch the suspect's body language (see page 88).

Hu. We hotfooted it to Hack's house. Oh, no! He was in the tub, lying so quiet and still under the shower curtain. Were we too late? Was it the Big Sleep for Hack, the Dirt Nap, the Long Goodbye? Then a loud snore fluttered up from under the shower curtain. Oh, good! It was only the Long Nap.

Homes started talking to Bubbles, telling him exactly what he did and when. "You hid in the shower, waiting for Hack. Big surprise when Hack flipped on the water and the dye on your pant legs started to run. He tried to talk you out of it, but you tied him up. You trashed his room to confuse us because you couldn't resist keeping his games. You're addicted! Look at those thumbs. They're from using the game controller 24/7."

But suddenly Bubbles grabbed Sam and jumped onto the windowsill. We were two stories up.

"Nobody move, or the dog gets it!" Bubbles yelled.

It was time to take a different tack. I started talking to Bubbles gently. "I know how you feel, man. Why wouldn't you bulk up and keep quiet when you feel scared and not in control? We're all outsiders. Remember how kids used to make fun of me, calling me four-eyes? Put down the dog before somebody gets hurt. We can work this out."

And then Bubbles let go of Sam Spayed and burst into tears.

Just The Facts

Here's the basis of my hypothesis. Go back to page 69 to find out how I put this all together.

- Cyn City School's computer database had been wiped out, taking everyone's grades with it.
- The screen savers BaddBoyz was handing out had subliminal images and strange codes on them.
- Hack had been kidnapped by a giant clown, or rather, someone dressed like a giant clown.
- The clown costume Bubbles used belonged to the Burp! Burger's mascot.
- The Burp! Burger wrappers were being sprayed with nanotechs and contained coded messages.
- Burp! Burger's and BaddBoyz were in business together.

Raymond Chandler's *The Big Sleep* and *The Long Goodbye* are famous hard-boiled detective novels.

Goodbye and All That

Hu. Burp! Burgers and BaddBoyz had cooked up an awful plot to take over Cyn City together. The nanotechs on the Burp! Burger wrappers would have turned everyone who touched them into video game addicts—with a special taste for BaddBoyz' games. The Burp! and BaddBoyz promotional screen saver was embedded with subliminal images that implanted an irresistible urge to eat more Burp! Burgers (even in vegetarians!). But that wasn't all—the screen saver contained a virus that, loaded onto a school computer, erased everyone's grades. Whammo—college prospects gone! Burp! Burgers would have all the low-wage employees it needed…forever.

Hack had figured this out (undoubtedly by hacking into the franchise's top-secret computer system, but he wouldn't admit anything when we asked). So Burp! Burgers and BaddBoyz bribed Bubbles Butler with free video games to kidnap Hack. They also pretended they'd make Bubbles a partner and add his name to the company logo: BBBBBBB. When he freaked and tried to back out, they threatened to cut off his game supply if he didn't cooperate.

Bubbles left the goodbye note to make Hack look guilty. His big mistake, besides not knowing how to spell, was the clown outfit. He thought it would disguise his identity, especially the telltale size of his thumbs. But when Homes noticed that the giant handprints in Hack's room were only five feet apart, he realized the kidnapper was normal-size.

Sylk and Penny were clueless. As usual. That mysterious call to the exterminator? Sylk was just trying to bug Pink. As usual.

If Hack hadn't pointed us in the right direction with his hidden messages, Cyn City would have become a burger-munching, video-game-addicted wasteland. Thankfully, we alerted the authorities just in the nick of time.

The school system offered The Pinkerton Detective agency a job as internal security. I was for it, until Pink pointed out, "Number one, we walk alone. And number two, who wants to rat on your classmates? Except maybe Sylk…"

Homes interrupted her before she could get any further. "I can't believe it took me so long to figure it all out," he said. "As anyone who's bothered to read a mystery would know, the Butler did it."

"But we'd look terrible in these hats!"

A Note from the Author

Whew. My three young detective friends were actually very unhappy when I told them they were running out of pages to tell the story of the time Hack disappeared.

So I promised they could add this Handbook.

Turn the page for more useful information on a detective's vocabulary, evidence collection techniques, and a list of things to read if you're serious about the craft— because one good book leads to another. Don't let the trail get cold!

—Janice

Make an Evidence Bag and Tape

A case is only as good as the evidence that supports it. You need a supply of paper bags and an official Chain of Possession form to keep your evidence safe. (Using paper bags keeps evidence that has moisture in it from molding or corroding.) Seal the bags with official tape, so nobody can tamper with the contents, and carefully maintain a record of who had the evidence after it was taken from the crime scene.

WHAT YOU NEED
- Templates
- White paper
- Photocopier (optional)
- Scissors
- Glue stick
- Plain brown paper bags
- Black fine-tip permanent marker
- Ruler
- Red or yellow crepe paper or plastic tape*
- Pad of paper
- Pencil
- Footlocker or closet you can lock

*Available at hardware stores.

WHAT YOU DO

1. Make photocopies of the Evidence Chain of Possession template above, sizing them to fit your bags. Cut them out and glue to the bags. Or, draw it directly onto the bags.

2. Using the ruler and marker, repeatedly copy the Evidence Tape template onto the crepe paper or plastic tape. Reroll the tape.

3. Practice collecting pieces of evidence in your room. Just about everything on a crime scene is potential evidence, including cloth, buttons, rope, tape, handwritten materials, tools, and broken bits of plastic or glass.

4. Mark the items with pieces of tape, your initials, and the date, if you can do this without altering or destroying the evidence.

5. Put the evidence in the bag, fold the bag closed, and glue a piece of evidence tape over the fold so the bag can't be opened without breaking the tape. Number the bag.

EVIDENCE

Case No. _____ Item No. _____ Offense _____

Date collected _____ Time collected _____ Collected by _____ # ____

Description of item _____

_____

Location where found _____

_____

CHAIN OF POSSESSION

Obtained from		By		Given to	Date	Time
Date	Time	Received from		By	Purpose/Reason	

Obtained from		By		Given to	Date	Time
Date	Time	Received from		By	Purpose/Reason	

Obtained from		By		Given to	Date	Time
Date	Time	Received from		By	Purpose/Reason	

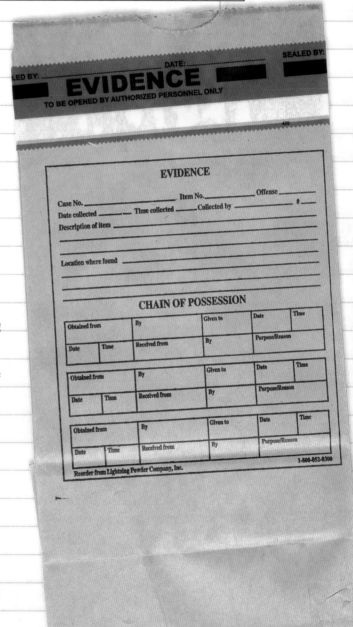

SEALED BY: _____ **DATE:** _____

EVIDENCE

TO BE OPENED BY AUTHORIZED PERSONNEL ONLY

6. Fill in the descriptive information blanks on the bag. As you do this, keep a written list on your pad of paper. Include the bag number, what's in it, when it was bagged, where, and the initials of the person who collected the evidence. This list is backup proof that the evidence exists.

7. Lock the bags in the footlocker or closet. Then, there's no question who has access to the evidence. If you mark, record, and store evidence properly, it can be used by the police in court.

8. When you hand over the evidence to someone else, fill in the Chain of Possession blank so there's a record of who had the bag and when. This is called "maintaining the chain of custody" or "chain of possession." Keeping this record is important, especially if evidence is tampered with or lost.

Secure the Scene: Crime Scene Tape

When you need to secure an environment under investigation, this tape is hard to miss.

WHAT YOU NEED

- Template below
- Piece of tracing paper
- Pencil
- Photocopier (optional)
- Sheet of acetate* (optional)
- Piece of thin cardboard big enough to accommodate stencil
- Scissors
- Large work surface
- Newspaper

- Roll of yellow crepe paper or fluorescent plastic surveyor's tape**
- Black craft paint
- Craft paintbrush
- Masking tape
- Quart-or gallon-sized plastic storage bag

*Available at office supply stores.
**Available at home supply stores.

WHAT YOU DO

1. Tracce the CRIME SCENE template with the paper and pencil or photocopy it onto a sheet of acetate. Carefully cut along the edges of the letters to make a stencil.

2. If you created a paper tracing, trace the letters again onto the piece of cardboard and cut them out to make a sturdier stencil.

3. Cover your work surface with newspaper, taping the sheets in place. Stretch one end of the crepe paper or plastic tape across the newspaper, tacking it firmly in place with bits of tape.

4. Position the stencil on top of the crepe paper or tape. Paint in the letters. Let the paint dry.

5. Move the painted portion off the work surface, "feeding" more of the unpainted portion of the roll onto the work area. Reposition the stencil and repeat the process, letting each portion of the crepe paper or tape dry before proceeding to the next.

6. When your crime scene tape is completely dry, roll it up and store it in the plastic storage bag.

7. Use the masking tape to attach your crime scene tape across doors, windows, and entryways. It comes in handy to keep people from bugging you while you're in your room, too.

Make a Fingerprint Database

Compile a database of fingerprints, so you can eliminate (or identify!) suspects at the beginning of an investigation.

WHAT YOU NEED

- Template below
- Scissors
- Black fine-tip permanent marker
- Ruler
- White index cards
- Photocopier (optional)
- Black ink pad
- Rag
- Fingernail polish remover
- Index card file box

WHAT YOU DO

1. Use the marker and ruler to trace copies onto the white index cards, or make multiple photocopies of the fingerprint form.

2. Write your subject's name on two forms or cards. Label the forms RIGHT and LEFT.

3. Working one by one, from thumb to little finger, touch one of your subject's fingers to the ink pad. Roll it gently on the card in the space allocated. Don't press or mash the finger or the print will smudge.

4. Repeat with the other hand, using the other card. Have them use the rag and polish remover to clean up.

5. Let the cards dry and file them alphabetically in the box.

Date	Finger	Hand	— Place Print Here —
Name			
Address			
Notes			
Prints Taken by:		ID No.	

Taking Footprints

Wherever you walk, you leave the imprint of your foot. We all walk differently, and our soles show different wear patterns. Cuts, gouges, and even gum or rocks stuck in the treads make shoe prints uniquely identifiable. Patent prints are visible, like when you walk across a carpet with muddy shoes. Make a patent print database from your family members' footwear and practice identifying distinguishing marks.

WHAT YOU NEED
- Newspaper
- Ink pad
- Brayer
- Shoes (Get permission to use other people's shoes.)
- Black fine-tip permanent marker
- Clean rags
- Rubbing alcohol

WHAT YOU DO

1. Spread out the newspaper. Apply the ink to the brayer.

2. Roll the ink onto the soles, and then press the shoe to the paper. Mark the print RIGHT or LEFT and identify whose shoe it is. Initial and date it.

3. Dampen the rags with the alcohol and use them to clean the soles thoroughly.

4. Make as many shoe prints as you can. Collect different pairs of shoes from the same person.

5. Compare the prints to each other. Do certain types of shoes leave similar tread marks?

6. Look for similarities in different shoes that the same person has worn. Can you find identifying marks? Are there places that the tread is worn away more than others?

7. Collect prints and match them to the impressions you've made.

Collecting Latent Prints

Latent prints are invisible. They're made when oil, dust, or grime on shoe soles transfers to hard surfaces such as wood, tile, concrete, or glass.

WHAT YOU NEED
- Flashlight
- Fingerprinting kit (page 22)
- Ruler
- Camera
- Notepad
- Pencil
- Clear adhesive contact paper

WHAT YOU DO

1. Survey your house and yard for latent prints. To find them, shine the flashlight at a low angle across hard, polished, or waxed surfaces, such as the kitchen or garage floor. Look near doorways. Check pieces of newspaper or papers on the floor.

2. Use your fingerprinting kit to dust for footprints the same way you dust for fingerprints (see page 23).

3. If you find a latent print, put the ruler next to it. Hold the camera directly over the print and photograph it.

4. Record the print's length and width. To collect the dusty prints, remove the backing from the contact paper and smooth the adhesive side over the print. Lift the contact paper and carefully press it against the sticky side of another piece of contact paper.

Casting Prints

Plastic prints are 3-D impressions left in mud, snow, or other soft substances. Learn how to make casts of plastic prints.

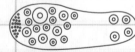

WHAT YOU NEED

- Shoes
- Dirt, mud, or sand
- Flashlight
- Camera
- Scissors
- Cardboard
- Duct tape
- Petroleum jelly
- Spray acrylic lacquer*
- Talcum powder
- Plaster of Paris*
- Water
- Clean, empty coffee can
- 1-gallon plastic storage bag
- Wooden paint stirrer
- Table knife
- Sand (optional)

*Available in craft stores.

WHAT YOU DO

1. Use different shoes to make 3-D impressions in soft dirt outdoors or in pans of dirt, half-frozen mud, or sand. Try tiptoeing, jumping, and stomping. Do they look different? Shining the flashlight from the side to highlight the impressions, photograph them.

2. Now you'll cast a print. Cut the cardboard into two strips measuring 12 inches long and 2 inches wide, and two more strips measuring 6 inches long and 2 inches wide. Tape the strips together without overlapping them to form a rectangular "frame" to hold the casting mixture. Apply the petroleum jelly to the frame's inner surfaces.

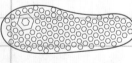

3. Lightly spray the shoe print with the acrylic lacquer. This strengthens the impression enough to support the plaster mix. Let dry. Sprinkle it with the talcum powder.

4. Press the frame in the dirt around the shoe print. Put the plastic bag in the can. Add the plaster of Paris and mix in the amount of water specified on the package. Stir to pancake batter–consistency.

5. Holding the wooden stirrer near the side of the frame, pour a stream of plaster onto the stirrer. Don't pour directly onto the impression or you'll destroy it. Never dump plaster in a sink; discard it in a trash can.

6. Let dry for 1 hour. Stick the knife into the ground at least 1 inch from the cast and gently lift up. Let the cast dry 24 hours, then brush off loose dirt. This technique can also be used for tire prints.

Tread-Mark Database

Collect all the wheeled items around your house (except the car) and make a tread-mark database. Tire marks can be important evidence at a crime scene, showing who was there.

WHAT YOU NEED
- Several large cardboard boxes
- Scissors
- Several bicycles
- Lawn chair or picnic bench
- Gloves
- Petroleum jelly
- Powdered paint
- Small, clean container
- White or yellow grease pencil
- Black fine-point permanent marker
- Rubbing alcohol
- Rag

WHAT YOU DO

1. Cut slots along the long sides of two or three large boxes; you'll use the boxes later to store your tread-mark database. Cut the other cardboard boxes into strips 6 to 12 inches wide, the length of each box.

2. Lay the strips end to end on the ground. You'll need several for a bicycle tire.

3. Elevate a bicycle by propping it on a lawn chair or picnic bench, so you can spin the wheels.

4. Wearing the gloves, mix together 4 tablespoons of petroleum jelly and 4 tablespoons of the powdered paint.

5. Use the grease pencil to make a large mark where you will start applying the mixture. Using your fingers, apply a thin coat of the mixture to the tire, going all the way around it.

6. Spin the tire so the grease pencil mark is at the bottom. Mark that point on the cardboard as the "STARTING ROTATION POINT" and then roll the tire along the cardboard strips, printing the entire tire.

7. Number the strips 1, 2, 3, etc., in sequence, and mark with the date, your initials, and which tire they came from: BICYCLE FRONT, for example. Set them aside to dry, and then file the strips by inserting them in the slotted boxes.

8. Use the rubbing alcohol and rags to clean the tires.

Tread-Mark Analysis

Make tire tracks with a friend and practice identifying them.

WHAT YOU NEED
- Roll of white shelf paper
- Hard surface, like a patio or driveway
- Rocks
- Dirt
- Water
- Several bicycles
- A friend
- Camera
- Ruler
- Magnifying glass
- Tread-Mark Database

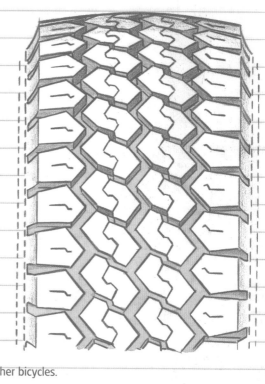

WHAT YOU DO

1. Lay a long piece of the white shelf paper on a hard surface. Put rocks on the corners to hold it down.

2. In a spot nearby, mix the water and dirt to make mud. Ride or push the bicycle through the mud and then along the length of the paper. On the paper, secretly mark which bicycle made the marks, set the paper aside, and put down another clean sheet. Repeat with the other bicycles.

3. Make more tread marks, running the wheels through dust, cut grass, or moist dirt.

4. Now have your friend photograph the marks with the ruler parallel to, perpendicular to, and running across the marks. Measure width and the length of the cuts in the tread. Record your measurements. Note any marks or flaws, such as a pebble stuck in the tread.

5. Now use the magnifying glass to match the shelf paper marks to the cardboard prints in your Tread-Mark Database.

How to Leave Invisible Messages

Are you about to be kidnapped like Hack? Here's how to leave secret messages for your fellow detectives. Note: Stash paper around the house so you'll have something to write on.

BARRICADED IN THE BATHROOM?

Steam Activated

Take a dry bar of soap and write on the bathroom mirror. Next steamy shower, the message will appear. This is good for telling somebody: QUIT USING MY SHAMPOO!

Plain Old Water

Use ordinary tap water as your ink. Brush the message onto a piece of paper with your finger. Let the paper dry completely. To reveal the message, dilute a teaspoon of regular ink in a glass of water, and brush it over the paper.

More H$_2$O

Soak a piece of paper with water and lay it on a mirror or hard countertop. Put another piece of paper on top, and write the message in pencil or ballpoint pen, pressing hard. Destroy the top copy. After the bottom copy has dried, its message will reappear when you wet the page again.

In the Medicine Cabinet

Does your dad keep a styptic pencil in case he cuts himself shaving? Wet it and use it to write your message. Heat will make it appear.

CAUGHT IN THE KITCHEN?

Sugar

Dissolve a few teaspoons of sugar in a glass of warm water. Write your message on a piece of paper.

Honey

Add a teaspoon of honey to a glass of warm water. Let it cool. Write your message on a piece of paper.

Baking Soda

Mix a tiny bit of baking soda with water. Write your message on a piece of paper.

White Vinegar

Use white vinegar as your ink. Let the message dry.

Milk

Pour some milk into a glass. Use the milk to write your message on a piece of paper. Allow extra time for your message to dry.

Cola

Add water to cola to dilute it. Write your message on a piece of paper. Let it dry.

Fruit

Collect juice from lemons, grapefruits, oranges, or apples by squeezing or poking them with something sharp. Use the juice to write your message on a piece of paper.

LOCKED IN THE LAUNDRY?

Laundry Starch

Mix $\frac{1}{2}$ teaspoon of laundry starch with $\frac{1}{4}$ cup water.

WRITE FAST!

Need a writing utensil? Look around you. You can use a toothpick. Sand the end of a wooden match until it's pointy. Use a nail from the junk drawer or an old, dry fountain pen, the kind with a pointy metal tip. Unbend a paper clip and use the pointy end. If you've got a small paintbrush, use it to paint the message. If you can't find anything to write with, use your finger.

REVEALING THE MESSAGES

If the kidnapping turns out to be a false alarm, take a look at what you wrote. To reveal these invisible inks, heat the paper. To warm it, you can iron the paper, put it on a cookie sheet and stick it in a 300°F oven, or hold it over a light bulb or radiator.

The Eyes Have It: Interrogation Tips

When you interview people, the truth can be hard to find. Suspects might try to mislead you, and even truthful folks can have a hard time describing things accurately. Physical clues and body language can signal that an interviewee might be fibbing—or that he's honest! You have to know how to read them. Try this with a friend. As the "suspect," he tells you (the detective) a story. Only the suspect knows whether it's a lie. The "detective" questions him, making notes of physical behaviors.

Nervous Nellies

Is the subject perspiring? Has his complexion changed in extreme ways, turning very pale or red? Is his Adam's apple bobbing up and down because he's swallowing a lot? Is he coughing or drinking lots of water? Does he fidget a lot with his hands, such as tapping his fingers, checking his watch or fiddling with jewelry? Does he have a tight grip on the chair or is he squirming around, crossing and uncrossing his feet or wiggling his toes? All of these clues can indicate he's nervous. The interesting question is, why?

Voice Patterns

Does the subject's voice sound tense? Are there sudden changes in his tone? Does he hesitate, or take a lot of time repeating your questions back to you? These may be hints he's hiding things or making them up.

Pants on Fire!

Watch the eyes. If a subject won't make eye contact, he's either being dishonest or is ashamed of something. Eyes moving to the right can indicate he tends to be outgoing and a people person but is still possibly saying something false. Eyes moving to the left means he's more of an introvert—but still a lying introvert.

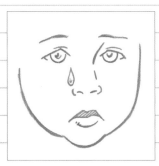

Eyes on the Eyeballs

Eyes can indicate honesty, too. When the subject looks up and into the distance after you've asked a question, he really could be trying to remember. If he looks at you with his eyebrows slightly raised for long periods of time while you're talking, he's interested in what you're saying. If someone is sorry about what he's saying, he often lowers his eyes. If he's sitting kind of slouched, with his legs spread out, and not looking you in the eye, he's ashamed of something.

Smiles, Real and Phony

When the subject smiles, does he smile broadly? He feels friendly toward you. Does the smile look forced, like it doesn't match with the eyes' expression? He's faking it.

Leave Me Alone

Posture speaks loudly without saying a word. Subjects under high levels of stress look tense. Is the subject standing or sitting, his hands in fists, arms crossed? He's feeling defensive. Intertwined ankles? He's withholding information. Sitting hunched over, chin lowered, eyes closed? He wants to stop, to withdraw. Shoulders raised closer to his ears than normal? He's afraid.

An Honest Joe

Square, straight shoulders and legs in an open, relaxed posture indicate an honest, responsible citizen. But if he pulls his shoulders back and tautens his neck, he's angry. Hey, what innocent person wouldn't be upset if he's accused of a crime, right?

  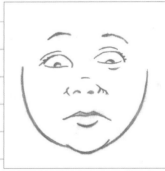

Fingerprinting with Superglue

The fumes from super glue react with body fat and oils to make "permanent" prints. This process is particularly useful when taking prints from plastic and metal. Always work in a well-ventilated area and avoid breathing the fumes—they're toxic.

WHAT YOU NEED
- Old pair of rubber kitchen gloves
- Clean plastic drink bottles
- Scissors
- Paper
- Cardboard
- Cloth
- Aluminum foil
- Craft stick

- Friends
- Latex gloves
- Wide-mouth jar with a lid
- Super glue*
- Plastic lid from a soda bottle

*Make sure the glue contains cyanoacrylate.

WHAT YOU DO
1. Cut the kitchen gloves and plastic drink bottles into small pieces (about 1 inch square) with the scissors. Do the same with the paper, cardboard, cloth, and foil. Break the craft stick into pieces.

2. Distribute the paper, plastic, cloth, foil, cardboard, and craft stick pieces among your friends. Ask your friends to collect skin oils on their fingers (rub their fingers in their hair or on the side of their nose), and then touch the squares to leave prints.

3. Put on the latex gloves and place the squares in the jar so the prints are facing up, with no overlapping edges. Fill the plastic lid with super glue and gently set it inside the mouth of the jar. If you're having trouble fitting your hand in the jar, turn the jar on its side and slide in the objects.

4. Screw on the lid, and leave the jar in a warm place for an hour. Check the squares and immediately photograph any prints.

Skulking

Sometimes you have to sit in one place and keep an eye on your suspect.

WHAT YOU NEED
- Somewhere to sit
- Book
- Snacks

WHAT YOU DO

1. Find a sheltered location on public property, like a bus stop or park bench. Take a book and keep a low profile.

2. Take snacks so you can eat without leaving your location. But you might want to restrict your water or soda intake so you don't lose your quarry during a bathroom break.

Newspaper Screen

Carry a newspaper on your surveillance mission. It's not just reading material—you can use it to hide yourself too!

WHAT YOU NEED
- Newspaper
- Pencil
- Scissors

WHAT YOU DO

1. Hold the newspaper in front of your face, so that it covers your entire face from view.

2. Use the pencil to mark a place on the newspaper level with your eyes.

3. Poke a hole through the pencil mark in the newspaper with the scissors.

4. Take the newspaper with you on your surveillance mission. Hold it up in front of your face and peek through the eyehole.

Inventing Codes and Ciphers

The simplest code to invent and use is to substitute one letter or symbol for each letter of the alphabet. Unfortunately, this simplicity means these codes can be easily broken—so check out the ways of complicating your codes below.

WHAT YOU NEED
- Black pen
- Paper
- Red pen
- Friend

WHAT YOU DO

1. Write all the letters of the alphabet across the sheet of paper with the black pen. Add any numbers or punctuation you'd like to use in your code at the end of the alphabet. (If your alphabet is longer than the page is wide, leave ½ inch between the lines.)

2. With the red pen, write a letter or symbol beneath each letter.

3. Make a copy of the code and give it to your friend (unless you want your friend to break the code in order to read your message).

4. To write a coded message, use the alphabet written in red ink.

5. To make your code even more difficult to decipher, use one symbol to indicate more than one letter, like the Mary Queen of Scotts cipher does:

Mary Queen of Scotts

A	B	C	D	E	F	G H	I	J K	L	M	N	O	P	Q R	S	T U	V W	X	Y	Z

6. Mary Queen of Scotts lost her head (literally!) because her code was broken. Use any of the following tips to make your codes more difficult to break.

   - Insert "dummy letters" between the real letters of your code. Try sticking them between every other letter, every third letter, or even in random places in your code.

   - Code your message. Then copy it backward onto a clean sheet of paper and destroy the original.

   - Code your message, and then group the letters into sets of three. Scramble the letters in each grouping.

Detectivespeak: A Vocabulary

As Sherlock Holmes says, "American slang is very expressive sometimes."

Bump off—Kill.

Chump—A stupid person.

Dame—A woman.

Detective story—Writer Anna K. Green created the term as a subtitle for her 1878 book, *The Leavenworth Case.*

Dick—Detective. Traced to the 19th-century English term, "to dick," meaning to watch, which in turn derived from the Hindu word *dekhna*.

Frail—A female, as in the "weaker" sex. I bet they never met Pink!

Gat—Rod, pistol, or gun.

Goon—A hired thug, derived from the Hindu *gunda*.

Gumshoe—Early 20th-century term for a detective, because gum-soled shoes allowed silent sneaking.

Gun moll—A gangster's female companion.

Hard-boiled—Description for tough World War I drill sergeants and the "real men" they produced. Later used to describe tough but good heroes in postwar detective fiction.

Joe—An average guy.

Mug—A foolish person, sucker, or sap, picked out by a criminal to attack.

Nuts—Another word for "no." Used since the 1920s.

Penny Dreadfuls—Short, sensational stories published in the 19th and early 20th centuries in England and the United States. After that came dime novels and pulp magazines, which featured mysteries and crime fiction.

Pinkertons—The agents of the Pinkerton Detective Agency, which was the first national (though private) U.S. police force before the FBI. They originally guarded the railroads and were called railroad dicks or bulls.

Private Eye—Private investigator, or P.I. Inspired by the Pinkerton Agency slogan, "The eye that never sleeps." Allan Pinkerton claimed crooks called him "The Eye."

Slammer—Jail.

Slang—Phrases used among criminals in the 18th century so police or potential victims couldn't understand them.

Tail—To follow someone without being seen.

The Essential Detecting Library: A Guide for Beginners

Since a detective's most important tool is his brain, make sure yours is well-filled. The immortal Holmes kept a scrapbook of interesting criminal cases around the world and referred to it frequently. He often solved cases by noting their similarities to earlier crimes. Whatever you can think of, you can probably find more about it in the library. These stories and books about crime and detection should definitely be on your reading list. Read the classics and learn from the masters!

Chandler, Raymond. *The Big Sleep*. Random House, 1992.

Chandler, Raymond. *The High Window*. Knopf Publishing Group, 1988.

Chandler, Raymond. *The Long Goodbye*. Knopf Publishing Group, 1988.

Chesterton, G.K. *The Innocence of Father Brown*. Wildside Press, 2004.

Christie, Agatha. *Masterpieces of Mystery and the Unknown*. St. Martin's Press, 2006.

Collins, Wilkie. *The Moonstone* and *The Woman in White*. Bantam Classics, 1985.

Dickens, Charles. *Bleak House*. Barnes & Noble Books, 2005.

Dickens, Charles. *Martin Chuzzlewit*. Penguin Books, 2000.

Dickens, Charles. *The Mystery of Edwin Drood*. Dover Publications, 2005.

Doyle, Arthur Conan. "A Study in Scarlet." *The Complete Sherlock Holmes, Volume 1*. Barnes & Noble Books, 2003.

Doyle, Arthur Conan. *The Complete Sherlock Holmes, Volume 2*. Barnes & Noble Books, 2003.

Hammett, Dashiell. *The Dain Curse*. Random House, 1989.

Hammett, Dashiell. *The Maltese Falcon*. Knopf Publishing Group, 1992.

Hammett, Dashiell. *Red Harvest*. Knopf Publishing Group, 1992.

Hammett, Dashiell. *The Thin Man*. Knopf Publishing Group, 2005.

Lincoln, Abraham. "The Trailer Murder." *The Black Cabinet*. Edited by Peter Lovesey. Carroll & Graf Publishers, 1990.

Poe, Edgar Allan. *Stories for Young People: Edgar Allan Poe*. Edited by Andrew Delbanco. Sterling Publishing, 2006.

Roosevelt, Franklin Delano et. al. *The President's Mystery Story*. New York, Farrar & Rinehart, 1935.

Sayers, Dorothy L. *Whose Body? A Lord Peter Wimsey Mystery*. Harper Collins, 1995.

Stevenson, Robert Louis. "The Rajah's Diamond." *The Works of Robert Louis Stevenson: New Arabian Nights; the Rajah's Diamond; the Suicide Club, Etc*. The World Syndicate Publishing Co., 1927.

Stevenson, Robert Louis. *The Suicide Club*. Dover, 2000.

Twain, Mark. *Life on the Mississippi*. Dover Publications, 2000.

Twain, Mark. *Pudd'nhead Wilson*. Dover Publications, 1999.

Twain, Mark. *Simon Wheeler, Detective*. New York Public Library, 1963.

Twain, Mark. *Tom Sawyer, Detective*. Tor Books, 1993.

Give Up? Cracked Codes

Page 12 Make Your Own Crime Kit
GRADES GONE HACK MISSING 3 DAYS

Page 32 Invisible Messages
Dear Three Friends No Time Eating Will Make You Sorry Hack

Page 40 Pigpen Cipher
EAT BADD BUY BADD PLAY BADD EAT BADD BUY BADD PLAY BADD

Page 41 Screen Saver Code
EAT BADD BUY BADD PLAY BADD EAT BADD BUY BADD PLAY BADD

Page 50 Time Is of the Essence
CYN CITY MALL SYLK BOUGHT A HAT NOTHING HAPPENING WITH THESE AIRHEADS

Page 55 Excellent Small Hiding Places
DEAR MAJOR HOTTIE FB I LOVE YOU I LOVE YOU I LOVE YOU BE MINE

Page 58 Color Codes and Secret Drops
FIND BUBBLES URGENT

Page 61 Book Cipher
DEEP # DOODOO # 4 # BUBBLES # BADD # AND # BURP # SAME # ADDRESS # 777 # MARLOWE # DR

Page 66 Coded Morse Message
BADD AND BURP PLOT TO POISON BURGERS CALL POLICE

Page 87 How to Leave Invisible Messages
I LOVE YOU FERNANDO!

Acknowledgments

I feel very lucky to work with the folks in the children's books division of Lark Books. They have had the wisdom to indulge this occasionally wild-eyed author her juvenile enthusiasms, shaped by long afternoons of reading hard-boiled crime fiction and Mr. Poe's gothic excesses.

Illustrator Jason Chin has done a beautiful job. Rain Newcomb, Joe Rhatigan, and Celia Naranjo, thank you for your professionalism and sense of humor. And welcome to the circus, Wolf Hoelscher.

I'm also grateful to my parents, Albert Koman and Marjorie Morgan Koman, for never interfering when I brought home books for which I was MUCh too young.

JEK

Index